PARENTING SCHOOL

CHILDHOOD AND ADOLESCENCE

Strategies for upbringing in a tumultuous world

DR. ANA KELLEYIAN

AND TEAM

ACKNOWLEDGMENTS

To the children we were and our current inner child.

To all children and adolescents who need adults to read this book.

To my son Matías, the driving force and endorsement of my work.

To the wonderful team of professional writers. People who make possible everything I cannot do and everything I do not know how to do. They are the team that never says no to my crazy dreams.

I mention them in the order in which I met them on the INEA staff.

Thanks to:

- Yolanda
- Gisela
- Ana María
- Stella
- Ariel
- Amorina
- Cyn
- Silvia
- Gustavo
- María

Ana Kelleyian
Compiler

INTRODUCTION

This is a book about children and adolescents but meant to be read by adults. Its goal is to provide basic assistance to those working with children and adolescents in schools, care centers, or even in their own homes with their children, nephews, godchildren.

The compilation was created by asking each professional on the team of the INEA Institute (Institute of Neurosciences, Education, and Assistance) to write about their area of work for the M.I.S.I.O.N. KIDS. This resulted in precise and direct contributions towards the objective. This book allows the reader to consult the compiler about doubts or questions on the website www.psicologaana.com.

We have tried to cover the main topics related to childhood and adolescence. Thus, this manual will be useful in every home, school, club, church, NGO, and other institutions. Therefore, we suggest it be accessible to all those who are caring for or intend to work with children and adolescents. We aim to cover as many areas as possible in the care, upbringing, relationship, and education of children and adolescents.

Adolescence has gained its place over the centuries. Thousands of years ago, according to the records found, we can affirm that children, and in some cultures women as well, were not valued. They were born, they existed, but they were not considered individuals. Only among the children of kings or pharaohs were firstborns of importance. Even in mythological legends, the children of gods were useful and entered history if they represented certain power, almost always granted or gained through cruel struggle.

Since the time of Genesis, one can read in each family's story, genealogy, and customs - how much the eldest son was valued, and how rarely other family members were privileged. Herod was the Pharaoh who ordered the death of all male firstborns to devastate the enemy population, and Herod's order also showed that children had no value. This was a means of controlling the growth of enemy nations and the world's population, so that Pharaoh and his nation remained secure.

When children were brought to Jesus, the disciples wanted those who brought them to keep them away from the Master. However, He allowed them to approach, and furthermore He stated that unless one receives the kingdom of God like a child, they will never enter it. (Luke 18:15-16). Just as Jesus recognized the woman as a person by giving her a place with attention in his ministry, so he did with the children.

2000 years ago, there were children, young people (around 30 years old), or adults on the social, familial, political, and religious scale. But the centuries advanced to also consider other age groups such as pubescents, the "older youth" and the old. Adolescents began to carve out a social space. Later, more specializations like "teenagers," preadolescents, millennials, centennials, older adults, the third and fourth age. The significance of all these emerging specializations is because human life has elongated and specified.

With this book, we will initiate the guide for working with children and adolescents. It will be used individually, within families, and in groups through interviews, workshops, or conferences. The same authors offer courses in different cities and countries through INEA International. They will be useful tools so that each of these chapters has its practical part.

From Conception to Adulthood

Life exists in parents before conception. That's why they cannot create anything other than life. Cysts, polyps, and tumors are all part of life. Every growing cell is alive. Within living beings, organisms develop and mutate.

In no way does the formation of a zygote egg cease to be life. The fetus is life.

Those of us who wrote this book believe in a person's life starting from conception itself.

What is M.I.S.I.O.N KIDS?

It is an organization that began in 2013 due to my visit to a children's home in the Province of Buenos Aires. My experience in Integral Health interviews or Inner Healing with adults for over a decade motivated me to do the same, with obvious differences, for children and adolescents.

So, I trained my first team for children. Through prayer, study, contacts, and experience, they learned and assisted me, eventually becoming specialists. They did an extraordinary job.

The court observes and monitors each case of each child through social workers, state psychologists, and psychopedagogues. Three months after treating the children, the director of the home calls me to say that the professionals from the state have noticed positive differences in the children's communication, drawings and tests, speech, and mood. They show me the report with a request: keep doing what you're doing for the children.

The minors needed us, not just to spend time with fun games, but also to talk, listen, and love them. The impact of seeing a 6-year-old child embrace a woman from our team in tears for over twenty minutes was so strong, I realized I must write this book to draw everyone's attention to the needs of children and adolescents.

M.I.S.I.O.N. KIDS stands for Ministry of Intercession, Inner Healing, and Prayer for Children. This is what we do.

Who wrote this book?

The authors are members of the Staff of the INEA Institute (Institute of Neurosciences, Education, and Assistance) in Argentina. Each of them professionally teaches and assists people of different ages or entire families, and they are specialists in their fields. This material is evidence of the skill and expertise of each professional.

However, this book could not have come to light without the work of Matías Emiliano Manoukian, who, with dedication, investment, patience, and continuous encouragement, managed to shape it.

I hope that whoever reads this book is blessed and uses the resources we provide on these pages to achieve efficiency in protecting and educating children and adolescents.

Ana G. Kelleyian

Ph.D. in Psychology – Neurotheologian

License No. 44431

Chapter 1

THE INTELLIGENT CHILD

Ana G. Kelleyian

Intelligence consists not only of knowledge but also the
skill to apply that knowledge in practice.
Aristotle (384 BC – 322 BC)

During the school years, a student with the best grades is called intelligent. Until a few years ago, children and adolescents underwent tests to measure their intelligence quotient (IQ). It was even assumed that those with higher IQs would perform better in life, and their future seemed assured.

However, if we pause to observe, we encounter situations like the following: the soccer "star," Lionel Messi, considered the best player today, delights us with his plays, making us exclaim "Genius!" What leads us to define him in this way?

In the Dictionary of the Royal Spanish Academy (DRAE), we discover that the word "intelligence" comes from the Latin "intelligentia," which in turn derives from "intelligere." This word is composed of two terms: "intus" ("between") and "legere" ("to choose"). Therefore, the etymological origin of the concept of intelligence refers to someone who knows how to choose: intelligence enables the selection of the most suitable alternatives for problem-solving. Later, we will analyze this in terms of "decision-making" in our brain.

Hence, the first meaning we find in the dictionary is "Capacity to understand or comprehend." The second: "Capacity to solve problems." And the third: "Knowledge, comprehension, act of understanding.".

Returning to Lionel Messi, when the footballer faces a situation in the game where it is necessary to elude opponents to reach the opposing goal, the "genius" has supreme skill in finding an option that solves the challenge.

Thus, the dictionary, which records the uses and customs for which terms are employed, anticipates this possibility. In its fifth meaning, we find: "Ability, skill, and experience." Generally, people who are highly capable in one area of their life do not necessarily exhibit intelligence in all areas. No one can be excellent at everything; those who specialize in a subject excel in that subject.

If every child is allowed to develop their vocation, supported and encouraged, they will overcome many, sometimes very difficult, obstacles. Talent is not enough: context (family, mentor, teacher, friends) confirms and empowers it.

Certainly, psychologist, researcher, and professor at Harvard University (USA), Howard Gardner, must have had something like this in mind when he formulated his theory of Multiple Intelligences in 1983. He included seven types of intelligence: verbal, logical-mathematical, spatial, musical, bodily-kinesthetic, interpersonal, and intrapersonal.

These intelligences work together, although as semi-autonomous entities. Each person develops some more than others (it's hard to imagine Bill Gates playing as a star striker or the Swiss tennis player Federer leading Steve Jobs' computer developments).

For example, "Bodily-Kinetic Intelligence" is the ability to process knowledge through bodily sensations (Lionel Messi, Rudolf Nureyev).

There are people who are highly skilled in logical-mathematical areas but struggle with interpersonal relationships, what Gardner called "Interpersonal Intelligence (social intelligence)".

It's "Intrapersonal Intelligence" that allows recognizing reactions, emotions, and inner life. Children and adolescents should learn to manage their emotions. Thus, adults must consider this as one of the essential aspects of education at home and at school. In several countries, it has been proven to start the day with a period of meditation (mindfulness), serenity, prayer: this allows both minors and adults to maintain calm in dialogue and efficient decision-making.

In some people, anxiety is extremely intense. They become so nervous before an exam or a choice that it interferes with their concentration and performance. Sometimes they even fall ill or give up the challenge, sabotaging what they could have accomplished splendidly. The body's autoimmunity defenses drop, stress kicks in, somatization[1] (the

---

[1] Somatization: definition from American Heritage Dictionary.

production of recurrent and multiple medical symptoms with no discernible organic cause) occurs. Generally, their most vulnerable part is affected. Headaches, teeth pain, breathing problems, stomach discomfort, acidity, palpitations, asthma, and more can be experienced. And all this, why? Due to a lack of cognitive intelligence? No, due to a failure in "Intrapersonal Intelligence.".

Sigmund Freud wrote an article titled "Those Who Fail to Succeed." This phenomenon is related to self-esteem, with the feeling that "it's too good to be true.".

Recent statistics in South America show that many adolescents do not receive a high school diploma because they leave pending exams and don't see the need to take them, assuming they won't pursue higher education.

There are people with high intellectual capacity who are unable to, for instance, choose good friends or a partner. Conversely, there are those less academically inclined who succeed in the business world, in sports, or in their private lives. All these areas require intelligence, but each requires a different type of intelligence. Not better or worse, just different. Scientist Stephen Hawking was neither more nor less intelligent than former basketball player Michael Jordan; it just happens that their intelligences excel in different fields.

All human beings possess the capacity to understand and engage with the world through different modes: language, logical-mathematical analysis, spatial representation, musical thought, physical use, nature, understanding others, and understanding oneself.

So, what sets humans apart? The intensity of these intelligences and the ways in which they are accessed and combined to navigate life and progress in different spheres.

However, all these can be developed to a greater or lesser extent. Thus, these differences challenge the education system that assumed everyone could learn the same subjects in the same way and that a uniform and universal measure was sufficient to test students' learning.

Therefore, today we know that what we call intelligence is not a simplistic, simple, or uniform phenomenon. Instead, it is complex and difficult to define. Modern psychology acknowledges the existence of different types of intelligence, the number of which varies depending on the author proposing them.

The brain and the mind are like a computer and its programs: one is visible, occupying space, and the other is virtual, modifiable. The brain and the structure of a child's mind complete their development outside the womb. In fact, the skull finishes closing as it exits the maternal womb. The need to remain open is due to the ability to narrow for passage through the birth canal. Similarly, vision, unnecessary in the womb, fully "adjusts" when at a greater distance from objects. The lungs and respiratory passages sense the air and begin to exhale, inhale, and yawn. The child enters the world with the "mental wiring installed," yet without utilizing the lights.

When a newborn perceives through its senses, basic "connections" begin to form in the brain. It learns to differentiate smells, colors, tastes, textures, sounds, and more. By the age of two, 80 percent of the brain is already functioning, which is why the early years are crucial for health, movement, comprehension, affection, learning, and more.

As the baby grows, so does the size of their body, skull, and brain mass, reaching adolescence with 1200 to 1500 grams of brain mass, depending on age, sex, and build. Sometimes it's said that children are like sponges, absorbing, grasping, and imitating everything they see. That's why the education they receive during these early years, through contact and context, is crucial, rather than academically.

The brain completes its growth by the age of 35, particularly in the prefrontal cortex, which is why decision-making and interpersonal function are not fully concrete during adolescence. The adolescent mind enters a confusion of roles between what is said, requested, and taught in different places and by different people. This makes them uncertain and troubled, leading to decisions without a basis and without considering consequences, often without knowing what they believe or want.

Education through Words

Education happens in many ways, all the time, especially with children, even unintentionally. However, words educate and miseducate. Everyday life and coexistence exert an unavoidable influence. This is why the way adults speak is crucial. Words will be repeated; respect for others is included in what is said, as well as the tone of voice, listening, gestures, timing, gaze, or impulsiveness in rhythm, among other expressions.

Children feel valued or despised in the family based on how they are spoken to. It's important to emphasize that listening to shouting, insults, or lies, especially within the family, triggers fear and insecurity in children. It diminishes their self-esteem and communication. Emotions are suppressed as the amygdala gets accustomed to repressing positive emotions. The cerebral amygdala[2] a paired structure (considered one brain area) inside your temporal lobe: a key part of emotional control and processes. It also plays a role in memory and learning is responsible for regulating experiences and emotions perceived as dangerous.

Recalling a moment as threatening, frustrating, or very difficult leaves a mnemic trace that will manifest as fear of something, someone, or a situation without being able to explain it, activating defense mechanisms and narrowing reason.

Let's suppose that a child is learning to ride a bicycle or play a video game, and this learning proves challenging. Enthusiasm and fearlessness can drive the child to keep trying until successful, without anger or self-reproach, with determination and even great excitement each time, if encouraged and supported in their effort. However, if parents become impatient, belittle them, shout, compare them, or offend them, the child will likely make a mistake, triggering fear. They won't want to try again, closing themselves off from the experience.

That fear that secretes cortisol will activate the stress hormone and the amygdala, so that they protect the child as a defense against the fear they feel. But, learning is also blocked and a defense armor is formed against screaming.

This memory, sometimes unconscious, prevents the child from developing that skill. A barrier to any learning that involves practice and patience is created. As adults, they will have to unlearn this mechanism and then relearn a new way of reacting or forming a habit, which can be challenging in adulthood.

Therefore, if you love children and adolescents and wish for their secure and independent future, you will take care of how you treat them and interact with others. How to face negative experiences without frustration and difficult moments without desperation is something they will learn from the behavior of the adults closest to them. They will accept challenges that require cognitive, action, or relational efforts in an atmosphere of love and patience. A child who associates their childhood

---

[2] Amygdala: definition from https://my.clevelandclinic.org

with happy moments will become a content adult, enterprising, and self-assured.

Chapter 2

Part 1

THE CHILD WE ONCE WERE

María del Carmen García

Human beings are born with a potential that develops in relation to the environment. The first bonds are established with the family, which is largely responsible for education and support during development.

To grow healthy intellectually and physically, for a good mental and spiritual process, every child needs to have role models they can admire and identify with. Those first referents are the parents, who transmit the inheritance and provide information about whether the world is a safe or dangerous place; what it is to love or hate, and based on this you learn to respect/yourself and value yourself, or to demand/yourself and mistreat/yourself.

With each client, therapists ask ourselves: where to start? And logically, beyond the reason for the consultation, we will investigate certain aspects of childhood, including an overview regarding their parents and family of origin, to find out what values they have held and, depending on the maternity treatment they have received, what memories it evokes of what that has been named for him/her.

When the baby says "mom"

Doctor Rene Spitz points out the acquisition of speech as the beginning of mental operations, in which the I acquires new functions such as *abstraction* and *reversibility*.

The forms used up to 18 months are different from adult communication: the child uses global words that express need; they represent phrases and are transitional. When the baby says "mommy" she expresses a whole range of needs, such as "I want to eat", "I want to see you", etc.

The only exception in verbal ability (from 10-18 months) is the negative gesture of cultural semantic communication: agreeing and refusing, tilting or shaking the head, are a clear indicator of abstract, ideational processes. The word "No" expresses only the negation, it does not represent an object; implies a greater degree of abstraction and judgment capacity. This gesture announces the development of higher intellectual functions and the use of them at the service of adaptation and skill.

Naming the mother is done "magically," while at the same time it implies establishing a distance. Later on, the mother ceases to be the source of language, but her laws are attributed to the father. Although language preexists the individual and is something to be acquired, this incorporation takes place in a play of identifications and passions.

We are born more than once

The biological birth of the infant and the psychological one do not coincide in time, as the latter is an intrapsychic process of slow progress.

Gestalt psychology, a school of psychology that emphasizes the wholeness and completeness of forms, informs us that we can deduce a figure from its still incomplete parts. Hence, it is observed that a 3-month-old baby is capable of recognizing faces in front of them and smiling. However, that same baby who offers a social smile at that age may cry inconsolably and hide their face from any unfamiliar person 5 months later.

This is known as the "eighth-month anxiety," which emerges when any human approaches, other than the mother or the immediate family of the baby. What has happened? Simply put, the newborn has been evolving psychologically. And while these behaviors may seem contradictory, they are completely normal and become integrated in the course of development.

This development comprises progressive changes that tend towards increasing complexity; those of quantitative order are referred to as **Growth,** and those of qualitative order, **Maturation.**

Identification

It is a psychological process through which an individual assimilates an aspect or attribute of another and transforms themselves either partially or wholly based on this model.

It encompasses a range of psychological concepts: imitation,

16

empathy, sympathy, mental contagion, projection. It is the most primitive form of emotional connection with the mother.

Authors like Bowlby in **Attachment Theory** refer to the concept of emotional bonds that people form with others throughout life..

Ainsworth, in **The result of a longitudinal study**, identified three types of attachment::

Secure: The child seeks protection and security from the mother. If she consistently provides this care, it allows the child to develop a positive self-concept and self-confidence.

Avoidant: The primary caregiver consistently fails to attend to the child's protective needs. As a result, children feel insecure and displaced by experiences of neglect.

Ambivalent: They respond to separation with great distress and often mix attachment behaviors with constant protests and anger.

Adaptation

From the very beginning, the child molds and unfolds within the matrix of the dual unity of mother and infant. The baby configures itself in counterpoint and harmony with the mother's ways and style. Its capacity to be shaped by the environment is present from birth.

In order to love, the child must 'construct' a whole person, and the first complete person the child develops is themselves. Difficulties in the constitution of their I leave traces that can lead to different pathologies, as humans are in constant interaction with the external environment.

Nevertheless, the child can experience anything from minor difficulties to severe abuses. That's why therapists inquire about how they resolved relationships with their peers in school, with their teachers; memories associated with words like fear, loneliness, or helplessness can emerge.

Concepts from Specialists

Children from 0 to 3 years

Dr. Margaret Mahler focused on *symbiotic psychosis* in children with panic due to the mother's absence. She refers to symbiosis as an intrapsychic state and posits that two factors influence development: a genetic one and a maternal one (a "shield" involving the mother-child dyad).

According to this author, development is a process of *separation-individuation* in two phases: symbiotic fusion (0-3 months) and achievements (4th to 36th months), with *sub-phases of Differentiation* (7 months); *Locomotor Exercise* (crawling and locomotion); *Reapproach* (15 to 24 months), early and personal; *Object Constancy* (24-36 months).

These developments can diverge from the normative sequence, experiencing delays or precocity. For example, premature locomotor development might occur before internal regulatory mechanisms provide the means to cope with that awareness. Alternatively, an omnipresent and infantilizing mother might delay the development of the Ego-Non Ego differentiation.

Dr. Donald Winnicott asserts that the Good Enough Mother satisfies the infant's primary needs and allows them to feel like a BEING when they see themselves in her eyes. She must provide:

1) The capacity for containment.

2) Physical contact with the body.

3) A sense of magic and omnipotence.

The **transitional object**, as described by *Winnicott* (1953), is *"a monument to the need for contact with the mother's body, expressed so movingly in the infant's preferred insistence on an object that is always the same, soft, flexible, warm to the touch, but especially demanding that it be saturated with bodily odors. The fact that the infant usually presses the object against their face near the nose likely indicates to what extent that object substitutes for the mother's breast or soft neck."*

When the mother is not integrated and reflects her own concerns (melancholic, depressive, psychotic), the baby then appropriates the maternal function and constructs a defensive shield (false Self) to protect their true Self. Later, they will attempt to be what they are not in order to please their parents and the external world.

When the baby separates their sensations from consciousness, **dissociation** occurs, leading them to satisfy their needs **symbolically** in adulthood (through alcohol, sex, drugs, compulsive shopping, money, or power).

According to Jacques Lacan, the Mirror Stage constitutes the matrix and outline of the Self. The baby achieves bodily integration in this phase, preceded by the phase of the fragmented or dismembered body.

The narcissistic bond is a relationship between two individuals in which the other is experienced as the one who completes. This bond with the mother is broken, and the discovery of the paternal relationship takes place. The presence of the father discourages the fantasy of this attempt at fusion. The triangular situation pushes the child toward the social, affirming the child's identity and allowing them to discover their individuality.

While the biological fact is being born male or female, psychic construction gives rise to masculine or feminine identity, and in this regard, the "triangular" situation with the father and mother is fundamental for asserting the child's identity and individuality.

Sigmund Freud referred to this preliminary period as autoeroticism, followed by the narcissistic stage, in which partial drives unify. The individual supposedly falls in love with their own image, as Narcissus (according to Greek mythology) fell in love with his own body reflected in the water.

The child from 3 to 6 years

Freud pointed out that the Oedipus Complex occurs between 3-5 years of age, during the *phallic stage* in which the child abandons their incestuous desires towards the parent of the opposite sex. Just as birth breaks the symbiotic bond with the mother, in this period, the psychological symbiotic relationship with her is broken, leading to the discovery of the paternal relationship. The presence of the father discourages the fantasy of this new fusion attempt, as he represents the third member and enables intrafamily discrimination. The triangular situation pushes the child toward the social.

Preschool stage. The next stage is referred to by developmental psychologists in various ways: *early childhood, phallic or Oedipal stage,* *preoperational intelligence, and intuitive thinking.* The child ceases to be seen as a baby, as they physically resemble an adult. The child will learn to formulate critical judgments about themselves, the world around them, and the situations they experience. Parents must help them in elaborating these judgments.

Latency stage. Regarding sexuality, the <u>Latency stage</u> occurs between 6-10 years, during which curiosity about sex shifts towards the acquisition of knowledge.

The child from 10 to 12 years old:

In this stage, there is a curiosity about sexual relationships as physical and psycho-emotional, spiritual, and social changes characteristic of adolescence begin to occur. It is very important here that children have clarity about the biological phenomena related to the gestation of human life.

Verbal communication should be encouraged, as they have developed the language level suitable for dialogue and prevention of potential risky situations. They should be shown the various realities that may arise so that they can analyze and consider strategies to resolve them. It's also important to teach them that impulses can be postponed.

In conclusion of this first part, it can be said that the insecurity of children manifests if the practical solution of love and setting limits does not work. Parents must prepare children and young people to face life, forming "antibodies" that allow them to defend themselves.

From an early age, it must be taught that every human action has a consequence, and they should be encouraged to take responsibility for their actions. This is the way to educate with responsibility, an essential complement to true freedom.

It's worth noting that just as there is no perfection in human beings, no parent is perfect, and thus, each individual must develop skills to recover from disruptive changes or misfortunes without being overwhelmed to the point where they act harmfully.

The greater flexibility and adaptability society requires, the more significant the family will be as a matrix of psychosocial development.

"...we have an initial individual action available: to investigate who we are, what has happened to us, and then determine if we can change something in favor of others..."
Gutman Laura *(2013).*

Part 2

Disruptive Adolescence: When To Encend The Alarm?

Lic. Silvia Waizel

In clinical practice as a psychologist specialized in adolescents, I observe that parents often request consultations in urgent situations. They come to the appointment distressed because they can't comprehend what's happening to their children. "My child has changed," "He/she wasn't like this," they argue. The truth is that these parents feel bewildered, as the changes in their children are not only physical but also in behavior and emotions. Additionally, they mention the discomfort within the family and the concern about how to move forward.

These parents realize that they no longer have the same flexibility they had during their children's childhood and find themselves overwhelmed by circumstances. It's evident that they have forgotten about their own adolescent crisis and view their children's experiences as something abnormal or akin to serious psychopathology.

These adolescents feel irritating, exhibit impulsive behaviors, don't obey, violate rules of coexistence, lying becomes habitual, they don't help with household chores, family arguments are frequent, and aggression and school absenteeism are common issues in consultations.

The question always arises: What situation are we facing? Is this typical of a "normal" teenager, is it a crisis, or is it a pathology?

This leads us to wonder when it's time to raise the alarm.

If we are to provide a simple definition of disruptive behavior, we could say that it's "antisocial behavior of one or more individuals characterized by a marked rupture from accepted general or social patterns of conduct and values. These behaviors can threaten harmony and even the survival of the group through hostile and provocative actions that incite the disruption of interpersonal and group activities."

What is commonly observed in clinical settings with adolescents is that antisocial actions or behaviors (discipline problems, hostile reactions, insolence, arguments, lack of commitment) are present as a means of processing anxiety (common during this phase) and generally escape the network of signifiers (impossible to put into words). Consequently, this clinical situation could be considered one of urgency or subjective urgency.

1. When should I consider that we are facing an adolescent crisis?

Nasio (2013) refers to crises affecting a "normal" adolescent, adolescents displaying "dangerous behaviors," and those "suffering from mental disorders." He mentions a drastic change in behavior, especially in boys, a reaction of systematic opposition that is unmanageable for parents and educational institutions. This sometimes intensifies abruptly through behavior that was potentially dangerous (a verbally aggressive youth suddenly erupting into physical violence against their father). This author suggests that an adolescent in crisis is one who is out of school, unemployed, frequently locks themselves in their room, is sometimes suicidal, obsessed with the computer/phone, or on the opposite extreme, wandering the streets.

This crisis puts the young person in danger, confounds parents, and causes distress in their environment.

Regarding young girls, they show a sudden depressive collapse, a profound discouragement that parents find unmanageable.

In boys, discomfort bursts outward and requires social institutions to provide containment. In "female adolescents," it implodes inwardly and necessitates careful listening by professionals. He adds that when young girls suffer, they seek protection, while when boys suffer, they expose themselves more than ever to danger.

The same author refers to "adolescent unconscious suffering," stating that adolescents don't always feel it and when they do, it's not clear, and if they do feel it, they don't articulate it. He adds that it is externalized not through ordinary adolescent fervor but through risky, impulsive, repetitive behaviors. Additionally, he notes that cruelty towards others masks a depression that isn't expressed through dejection and sadness but through "hostile depression."

These adolescent sufferings often also manifest through the body: cuts (especially on the arms, legs, and abdomen), anorexia, fainting. They say, "I feel better when I see blood." Do they feel that bleeding is a type of cure for other pains or an expulsion of the unbearable? Are they seeking pain to feel alive?

According to Urribarri (2015), these young individuals make changes in clothing, attire, and their bodily appearance; engage in physical practices not accepted by parents or somewhat risky; and, to a lesser extent, embrace brands, tattoos, and piercings to stamp their personal mark, asserting their ownership of the body and consequently using it as they please, in direct challenge to parental dominance and as a rupture and distancing from the child's body. Gestures, complaining faces, expressions of annoyance and rejection, vocal tones, and curt responses are clearly perceived, using terminology and teenage verbal codes in vogue, combined with bodily expressions as a way of differentiation from adults.

Thus, one might think of anxiety, sadness, depression, hatred, self-harm, expressions of annoyance and rejection, risky behavior – all as manifestations that serve as the tip of an iceberg, leading us to analyze what is happening internally and expressing itself outwardly.

2. Adolescent Crisis: A Parental Crisis?

Mannoni, Deluz, Gibello, and Hébrard (1984), referring to Louis de La Robertie, add, *"If there is a crisis in adolescence (a crisis of adolescence), there is also a parental crisis, and both are correlated... The adolescent cannot emerge from their crisis without the parents' difficult journey. And since parents can stumble on that path, it's to be expected that the psychoanalyst be with the adolescent."*

This underscores the importance of the presence of parents in moments of crisis (with successes and failures) and the crucial accompaniment of the analyst in the process.

Considering adolescence is to consider discomfort, which involves the adult world. Understanding this helps us be prepared and attentive. Discomfort can transform into depression or certain forms of behavior that disrupt family relationships and school matters.

Janin (2019) warns that when parents try to shield their children from every possible twist of fate, they leave them unprotected in the world, unable to explore new territories. Alluding to Winnicott (2004), he states that adolescents must "kill off the parents of childhood without killing them." In other words, parents must cease being omnipotent parents, yet it's crucial that they continue to exist and there's a space for confrontation. "Growing up means occupying the parents' place," and in the unconscious fantasy, growing up is an aggressive act. Moreover, parents must "survive," which is very important considering that we know some parents abdicate their role, as if they were dead in the face of adolescent attacks. And if the parent is dead, there's no one to confront. Thus, the adolescent can be left in a situation of extreme guilt, paralyzed, or enter into violent outbursts, attempting to bring the other back to life.

In this manner, it must be considered that being parents during this life stage is a role that, at times, won't be rewarding because conflict and confrontation are necessary and might not be simple at all.

3. Normal Adolescence Syndrome

Aberastury and Knobel (1988) make reference to the *"normal adolescence syndrome"* and assert that this *"largely results from the processes of identification and mourning that the adolescent may have undertaken... to the extent that they have worked through these mournings, which lead to identification, the adolescent will see a better-fortified internal world, and thus, this normal abnormality will be less conflicting and therefore less disturbing."*

The same authors mention a series of anticipated symptoms in adolescence, including successive contradictions in all manifestations of behavior, dominated by action, and constant fluctuations in mood and emotional states. Also, constant forms of expression within expected processes (mourning, disidentifications and identifications, exogamous love, new relational bonds).

Furthermore, they express that adolescents cannot maintain rigid, permanent, and absolute behavior, although they often try and seek it. It is the adults who cannot tolerate these changes in adolescents, nor eventual, transient, and circumstantial identities, demanding from them an adult identity they need not uphold.

Among these disruptive behaviors affecting this age group, we could mention running away from home. Dolto (1990) calls it a brief departure. The same author adds that running away is impulsive, cutting the knot of crisis without resolving anything, with no other objective than to escape what has become unbearable and impossible for the adolescent to face.

Reference is also made to "adolescents in crisis situations," with the following character traits: instability, hyper-emotionality, and emotional immaturity. Furthermore, several factors can contribute to running away, with the family environment playing the most significant role. Lack of parental understanding, family communication issues, violence, absence of authority, overprotection, and rejection are some factors that may lead to running away from home. Most of the time, running away is a solitary act resulting from unsatisfied emotional demands.

Adolescence entails risks, and if we wish to envision a peaceful adolescence, we would be denying the generational confrontation characteristic of this phase.

In conclusion, the problems, confrontation, boundary-crossing, impulses, and many disruptive behaviors that manifest during adolescence need to be analyzed and worked on. However, the presence of such behaviors doesn't necessarily indicate a disorder.

In this stage, there will be multiple passing crises that we shouldn't prematurely pathologize. Attributing adolescent issues to biological causes and rapidly medicating is to perceive them (young boys and girls) outside the psychic and social framework that shapes them (Janín, 2019). We cannot solely focus on the external aspects of their actions, disregarding the family historical baggage they carry.

These adolescents are growing and facing countless changes that trigger crises. Sadness over what's lost, anxiety over the uncertain. Within these vicissitudes, many demands come into play, not all of which can always be met. "Sexuality poses new demands, and narcissism must find new supports" (Janin, 2019).

We observe that crises, manifested through disruptive behaviors, will always be present. They constitute an unconscious suffering that can't be put into words and is externalized through risky, impulsive, and repetitive behaviors. Generally, if there's an adolescent crisis, there's also a parental crisis, where tragedy and suffering are present. It could be termed a normal crisis of adolescence, where emotional instability plays a significant role.

It would be a utopia to expect young boys and girls to exhibit permanent and absolute behavior. It's also important to recognize that growing up, for them, is an aggressive act, from which parents must emerge intact.

Furthermore, the manner in which they navigate their adolescence will depend significantly on whether the context offers them a space of narcissistic support. At this juncture, the work of parents is paramount.

Let's bear in mind that, when in doubt and concern about our children's well-being, we shouldn't wait too long. A timely consultation can save much pain and uncertainty. Undoubtedly, the therapist will guide and equip you with the necessary tools to navigate this period, which will become part of history.

Chapter 3

LIFE AND DEATH

Gustavo Romero – Ana Kelleyian

LIFE

Explaining to children or adolescents how babies are born and when someone dies is very different. Respecting their cognitive age and addressing the specific questions of each child or adolescent is best. Minors might ask their parents or siblings, but they might also inquire with cousins, teachers, leaders, peers, or their friends' parents. Therefore, when faced with doubts or questions, let's briefly respond with some general information and inquire about what information the children and adolescents have and what they specifically want to know.

Next, we need to ascertain whether the doubt originates from their own imagination or from something they heard or were told, and who said it. Many times, children and adolescents cannot process information well because they lack clear foundations. The mind tends to fill in the gaps in partial information received, and the questions they ask are usually not well-constructed.

Explaining Life

Nature, the planet, the universe, God – these concepts, much like the image of a circle, a mother, the Earth, are unconscious ideas that seem to be imprinted in the mnemic trace of newborns, which still isn't fully understood. Childhood is an ideal time to plant these absolutes in the mind. Thus, parents, guardians, and authorities (school, church, grandparents) will almost unwittingly instill these ideas in children..

Gestation and birth further solidify this notion. Almost no one explains to children using "strange" figures (storks, cabbage, little plants, angels) how babies come into the world (or at least, that's what I hope). Sometimes, in our desire to be brutally honest with our children, we tell them things that will only confuse them more or that they can't yet comprehend. Often, they'll turn to others with their doubts, and not everyone explains things the way parents would like to. That's why it's so crucial to be attentive to children's questions and respond with simplicity.

Sometimes, they might not be siblings in the strictest sense, but they could be cousins, siblings of friends, or neighbors. A newborn baby doesn't go unnoticed by adults or children. Of course, discussing this with adolescents will be different, presenting a valuable opportunity to talk about sexuality, pregnancy prevention, and sexually transmitted diseases. The aim should be to avoid instilling fear or repression. Instead of framing it in terms of restrictions or freedoms, parents should guide their children on values and boundaries.

For teenagers who are still learning about life, encountering death raises more questions than it might for an adult. This is because adults are more conscious that time cannot be regained, and age brings them closer to death. On the contrary, for a teenager, death seems like something that will always happen to someone else and not to them.

The world has changed. Society has changed. The youth has changed. Yet, fundamental needs and necessities persist. Social media (as the name suggests) have brought people closer together, breaking down distances and granting us control over information. We now know who went where, with whom, for how long, how their time was spent, where they dined, how much they spent, and whether they enjoyed the experience. In some ways, we can consider this evolution.

These changes have two facets: on one hand, they are abrupt. What is today might not be tomorrow. The brain, with its elasticity, must adapt to new concepts and paradigms that technological migrants may struggle to comprehend; and when they do, new changes occur. Implicitly, this carries the other facet: speed. Within a single day, news from the other side of the world can redefine the socio-economic landscape of where we are at that moment.

Adolescents – who are digital natives – don't just adapt to this new reality; they are the new reality. Technology – and its wealth of information – adjusts to them, to their speed, reading capacity, decision-making abilities, and needs. However, considering that they are still in a formative stage, what are the consequences of technology's arrival during an age when certain aspects, such as sexuality, the true implications of death, or the consequences of actions, are not fully defined?

The very word "adolescent" refers to who they are and who they aspire to be; it's a time of life marked by searching and change, especially in terms of sexuality and social interactions. This period can be roughly divided (though not universally applicable) into early adolescence, spanning approximately from ages 9/10 to 14. This stage is mainly characterized by the onset of puberty – a phase involving significant physical changes related to growth and sexual maturation, accompanied by corresponding psychological shifts. Following that is mid-adolescence, from ages 15 to 17, characterized among other things by family conflicts due to the system's increasing importance, as well as school problems and bullying, which is essentially a power dynamic among peers. Finally, late adolescence occurs between ages 18 and 21, marked by the reacceptance of family values and concepts, and by the assumption of tasks and responsibilities associated with adulthood (or the conflict arising from not being able to assume them).

Adolescence is a stage of questions and the fear of not finding answers; it's a time of familial and societal pressures. It's the gray area where the struggle is both external and internal. In this phase, while still shaping the concept of one's identity, the ability to stand up to the world and defend oneself is often lacking. This is where external stimuli play a significant role.

The internet has desensitized us. Let's recall when we were children and a kiss in a soap opera might have prompted our parents to cover our eyes. Now, such scenes can be freely viewed, at any time and at any age, even the most horrifying of crimes, hardly surprising anyone. And least of all teenagers, who seem to actively seek out this kind of visual information.

The age when reading was the source of knowledge and a gateway to a universal worldview is long gone. For today's adolescents, reading is burdensome, tedious, and tiring. The time when reading sparked imagination and entertainment has passed. Nowadays, everything is within sight – just a swipe away, influenced by a friend's opinion or that of a stranger on the other side of the screen. Their minds are bombarded with information transmitted through images; and the saying "*a picture is worth a thousand words*" has never been more apt.

If life is a question without an answer, and it's so painful due to its shortcomings, pressures, and lack of understanding, why live it? Let's escape from it!

In some cases, death is presented as an alternative. Death isn't just physical disappearance; it's when the desire to be alive dies first, the desire to move forward, to find meaning in existence.

In this context, **self-harm** has become a common practice among adolescents; it's an indicator of the conflicts they're going through. Self-harm can manifest as self-inflicted marks, hits, or cuts. This is also known as **parasuicide**, as the individual doesn't wish to cease to exist; rather, they want the problem to stop bothering them. However, excessive self-harm can lead to death.

The pain of not fitting in, not belonging, and not enduring drives some individuals to seek physical pain, which paradoxically generates a sense of calm and even emotional relief. Yet, this is often followed by guilt and shame, causing the painful emotions to return, thus adding a new layer of emotional pain to the original struggle.

Child and Adolescent Suicide

Not all adolescents are grappling with deep issues that emotionally destabilize them to the point of making drastic decisions. They don't all manage emotional pain in the same way or experience the pain they face with the same intensity. However, a significant percentage cannot endure it. In fact, suicide is the second leading cause of death among individuals aged 10 to 19 in Argentina, as per a report presented by UNICEF in 2019. This trend is also observed in Latin America. But beyond statistics, it's crucial to understand that they view this as a relieving escape from their problems. They don't want to end their lives; they want the torment of their problems to cease.

The expectation from adults is that adolescents will speak up and share their problems. However, here lies the challenge: adolescents do talk about their problems, but not always verbally. Their behaviors, silences, isolation, rebelliousness, outbursts of anger, and more are not just ways to express their emotional state but also pleas for help.

Adults have the obligation to be preventive agents. There's a role that often remains vacant in today's families, that of being true parents. Parenthood isn't just about bringing a child into the world; it involves being a role model, showing empathy, setting boundaries, and fostering open dialogue from childhood. As a child grows, their independence increases as they test their strength in facing the world alone. They begin to rely less on their parents' opinions and start using their own judgment. This is one reason why pre-adolescents often don't communicate with adults. They see adults as "outdated" and old-fashioned, and to some extent, they have a point.

This gradual decline in dialogue creates a rift precisely when adolescents need to talk and be heard the most.

Although this phase is inevitable, we can make it as beneficial as possible for both the adolescent and the parents through prevention, making dialogue an integral part of family routines. One of the key steps is to realize that devices and activities can consume the time that should be invested in conversations with our children. Sometimes, we assume that kids need English classes, volleyball, swimming, or a mobile phone, when what they truly need are parents who are ready to listen. Parents who can sense something is bothering their child with just a glance. Parents who won't judge them, who are open to giving a hug rather than a hasty punishment.

Abortion

There are different types of abortions: broadly speaking, we can categorize them as spontaneous, induced, and therapeutic.

A spontaneous abortion occurs when an embryo or fetus[3] dies without external intervention (medical procedures, medications, nurses, etc.), due to natural causes, and before the 20th week of gestation. Induced abortion is the voluntary termination of a pregnancy. Therapeutic abortion, on the other hand, involves ending a pregnancy due to the risk to the mother's life or when the fetus has genetic anomalies or severe malformations that would compromise its future life.

Regardless of the cause of abortion, it will have consequences for the woman or adolescent involved.

The term "abortion" brings to mind a political and social divide that the world is currently experiencing. Some people are in favor, while others are against it. However, the intention here is not to judge, but rather to consider what leads to the introduction of the abortion topic into the past, present, and future lives of adolescents.

Looking at the past, if an adolescent must contemplate abortion, it's likely because they are sexually active (unless the case involves abuse). This signifies an encounter with pleasure at the expense of responsibility.

---

[3] An embryo is considered when the gestational age is less than 8 weeks. Once it passes 8 weeks and until birth, it's referred to as a fetus.

At this point, we're not referring to information, as it's abundant and readily available to them just like any adult due to the internet and conversations with peers. We emphasize the role of adults in providing guidance and support throughout this process.

Adolescents often make significant decisions like these with little real awareness of the physical, psychological, spiritual, emotional, and even economic consequences of their actions.

But is it really so serious if an adolescent becomes pregnant? If the pregnancy is unintended, her own psychosocial development process is interrupted to care for another being. She hasn't fully defined her *"who am I?"* only to be faced with the response, *"I am someone responsible for a baby."*

Gone are the times when sexual activity was solely considered reproductive (except for certain groups today). However, as a society, we tend to swing between prohibition and encouragement. It used to be frowned upon for a young woman to engage in sexual activity before her wedding night; now, it's seen as strange or suspicious for someone to be a virgin before the age of 21. This places social pressure on adolescents within their peer groups. While hormones may drive a need for intimacy at that age, crossing the boundary of "no" isn't always because they want to, but sometimes because they feel they "must" to avoid being excluded. This pressure, coupled with a lack of information and impulsiveness, can lead to unintended pregnancies.

Parents often assume that their children "already know everything." The excuse *"they talked about it in school"* is a common refrain. But what do our children really know? Why do we assume that the information they received aligns with our values? We need to once again be preventive agents. We should ask ourselves: What do I think about this topic? What does my spouse think? What are the values we uphold in our home? Are we transmitting those values to our children?

However, if an abortion has already occurred, parents must not cease to be real parents. Despite the pain, questions, and guilt, we're obligated to strengthen our daughter's life.

During this time of grief, it's crucial to be empathetic, not judgmental. Putting ourselves in the shoes of the adolescent and feeling what she feels can aid the process. The goal is to encourage the adolescent to confront the pain, to express it, as feelings during this phase can include guilt, anxiety, distress, depression, decreased self-esteem, and suicidal tendencies.

Later on, there will come a time when it's necessary to reevaluate the values by which we've lived up to that point – perhaps a time when we, as parents, have inadvertently let things slide. What are we going to do today to change this reality? Are we going to let political currents, trends, or friends shape our children's values? Are we willing to face the consequences of their actions that have been influenced by our lack of parental involvement?

Regardless of the family situation, we always have the opportunity to take control of parenthood and steer things back on track. It's never too late to seize the reins of parenting and redirect the course.

Death

I remember, when I was a child, around 7 years old, Don Alberto, a neighbor of our house, passed away. It was a summer afternoon when it was common to ride bicycles without any supervision as it was a safe time. The tradition - and it still continues in some villages - was to have the wake at the deceased person's house. I have imprinted in my memory the atmosphere of crying and grief from Don Alberto's wife, his mother, and his son. But what pierces me is the memory of seeing myself crying on the sidewalk... when I hardly even knew Don Alberto!

At the age of 7, there isn't a real understanding of the meaning of death. Moreover, life - understood as existence - is taken for granted. Death is an inherent part of life. The thought of ceasing to exist doesn't fit into conscious thinking. However, whether or not we have experienced the loss of someone close or significant, children are exposed to countless pieces of information about death.

Just as in my case, in the past, this information was obtained through the passing of a family member, a neighbor, school, or why not? An animal or pet. Death was a taboo believed to be kept away from children as a form of protection. However, today's children live with death. It's on all of our lips when we talk about insecurity, in their internet games (where the objective is to kill the other). Nevertheless, having information is not a guarantee that the concept they have formed about it is correct or beneficial for them.

Children form their understanding of what death is through bits of data, ideas, and loose information they hear in their everyday environment, based on their fantasies and depending on their age and developmental stage. Keeping this in mind will help us have conversations with them, support them in the process if needed, and address any questions they may have. The language used to explain death to a 4-year-old is not the same as when explaining it to an 8-year-old.

The Concept of Death in Childhood

Children from around 6 months of age develop one of their first fears, which is the weaning process and separation from their parents. When we play with them by covering our faces and disappearing, asking them *"where is the baby?"* and then reappearing saying *"here I am!"* we don't realize the distress it causes in them. However, by playing this game and creating the idea of "not being there," we contribute, among other things, to the development of the concept of death. This also happens with changes in behavior and emotional changes in those around them, changes in routines, and relocations. These are the losses and changes that they discover through their senses.

Between the ages of 2 and 5, they perceive death as something not permanent. As sleep is an essential part of their routine, they believe that the deceased is just sleeping and will wake up to continue their normal activities. Just as sleep marks the transition from day to night and vice versa, the concept of time emerges when linked to specific events; there's an understanding of morning, afternoon, and yesterday. Additionally, they do not yet comprehend what the future is.

Since penalties or punishments are often related to separation (whether physical or taking away a toy), they might develop the concept that death is a punishment for bad behavior.

Around the age of 5, they begin to perceive death as permanent but only happening to elderly people. They assume that only grandparents die, not young people, let alone their peers. On the other hand, death is distant; it only happens to people who aren't close to them.

Around the age of 7, they have a clearer concept of time and recognize "today," "yesterday," and "tomorrow." It's important to note that their understanding of their body, organs, and their functions deepens. This is crucial as it aids in understanding the reasons behind a death.

Around the age of 9, they universalize death, understanding that it can happen to all living beings, including their parents and themselves. Movies and religious festivities contribute to personifying death as a grim reaper, a skeleton, or a black-caped figure with a scythe.

After reaching 8 or 9 years old, they already know that death is definitive, universal, and permanent: definitive because it happens once, universal because it applies to all living beings without exception, and permanent because there's no coming back from it. Their understanding of time, cause, and space is now developed, reinforcing the concept of death. This provides a valuable framework when discussing this topic with them.

Only after the age of 12 does their thinking become more adult-like, and they start forming ideas about the existence after death.

As adults, we need to understand that death is an abstract concept that isn't always easy to explain to children. Children might have numerous questions based on what they saw or heard and may not be able to express them using the right words. In our attempt to explain, we might unintentionally introduce concepts into their imagination that could generate fear, causing nightmares and fears related to family members and paralyzing inaction. Therefore, it's important to understand the child's cognitive age and individual level of maturity in order to provide explanations in the simplest way possible.

But then, what is death?

Setting aside the Christian concept of death, we can say that it's a permanent, irreversible, and definitive state. Why do we say that we're setting aside the Christian concept? Because Christianity, in all its facets (Catholic, Protestant), transcends this concept by having Jesus who triumphs over death itself, nullifying these three stages with resurrection.

If we look at video games and cartoons, there's always a character who dies: no matter how innocent the cartoon, death is present. The character appears in the next episode or the next round of the game as if coming back to life. Phrases like *"my phone died"* or *"what they said killed me"* are common for us. However, children might perceive death as timeless and reversible.

There are well-intentioned phrases that we shouldn't use without explaining that it's final, it's forever: *"They passed away," "They're in a better place now," "They're in heaven with God," "They're sleeping."* These phrases might arise in the midst of the child's own pain or out of ignorance, but they can create unrealistic expectations in them, such as the idea of a return. When they ask questions, we must clarify that the deceased do not come back.

Regarding the universality of death, as mentioned before, the concept at a certain age is that only the elderly die. The fantasy might also be created that only the "bad" people die (as seen in video games). Universality implies that everything with life (human, plant, or animal) will die at some point. Death isn't selective; it comes for everyone.

This adds the element of time. If it comes for everyone, when will it happen? Can it happen to me? Can it happen right now or while I'm asleep? Can Mom or Dad die? To answer these questions, we must consider why the child is asking them. What internal fear prompts those questions? What did they see or hear? Secondly, we don't always have to provide answers; sometimes, we should let them express themselves, let them voice their true fears. And most importantly, provide them with a sense of security. We might not have all the answers, but we can create an environment in which they feel comfortable, supported, and aware that we're there for them. A useful tactic is to observe nature with them, such as the life cycles of plants.

There is a physical cause:

Adriana couldn't fall asleep. She underwent medical treatments, used medications, tried hypnotherapy, but nothing worked. She spent nights awake without knowing why. She felt tired enough to go to bed and immerse herself in a deep sleep, yet she couldn't achieve it. After several sessions, she casually mentioned a family story: her newborn brother had died from sudden infant death syndrome while sleeping. Although she didn't know her brother, his name was mentioned at every family gathering. Adriana grew up with the story of the child who "fell asleep and never woke up."

Sleeping, having an accident, or falling ill are not necessary causes of death since we all sleep, experience accidents of varying severity, or get sick. Within this context, there are phrases we shouldn't tell our children without clarifying that this happened to that person at that time and is not true for everyone: *"He fell asleep and didn't wake up," "He died because of an accident," "He died because he got sick."*

Sometimes, and depending on the age, it's better to explain that certain organs in the body stop functioning or vital functions cease. We'll explore this further with examples related to cancer.

Every expression triggers an emotional response in children, for instance:

Lo que expresamos	Lo que provoca en los niños
Tu papá se fué al cielo porque era bueno	Confusión : *Si me porto bien me llevan..* Miedo a portarse mal. Miedo a quedarse dormido.
Se quedó dormido. Ya no va a despertar mas	
Esté donde esté te manda besos	Sentimiento de abandono
Tu papito se fué a un viaje muuuuuy laaargo....	Falsas expectativas de regreso. Ansiedad.
Dios la quiso tener a SU lado.	Dios egoísta.
No estoy llorando, se me va a pasar, andá a jugar.	Represión de sentimientos.
No tenes que llorar *No tenes que estar triste* *Hay que ser fuerte* *Llorar no es de varoncitos* *Ahora sos el varon de la casa y portate como tal*	Encapsular la libre expresión de emociones. Responsanbilidades no acordes a su edad. Cortar su proceso de duelo.

Now, when facing an event, how does grief manifest in children?

Catalina's parents decided to leave the city of Buenos Aires in Argentina, seeking a better future for their family. They chose to move to San Martín de los Andes, a small and beautiful tourist town in Patagonia. They had a beneficial job offer and Catalina's enrollment was confirmed at everything seemed perfect! However, after a while, Catalina started to become rebellious and moody. Her moodiness disrupted the family's peace.

When we talk about grief, we often associate it with death. However, when it comes to children, we must understand that grief can be triggered by any significant loss. This could include the absence or death of a close person, an unexpected change, or the loss of a cherished object. While an adult can easily replace a lost toy by buying another, for a child who has formed an emotional attachment to the object, it becomes a grieving process that generates distress. Moving away from a cousin, a friend changing schools, or having a different teacher are all reasons for loss that can affect a child's emotions.

The grieving process in a child's mind can be partially compared to the grieving process experienced by adults, with some expected reactions for the situation. In adults, these stages are generally as follows:

CRISIS: The news is received. There's emotional confusion and physical reactions like fainting.

DENIAL: Non-acceptance of the event, disbelief that it's real. Sense of unreality.

ANGER: A search for someone or something to blame, feelings of injustice, and questioning like "Why me?" or "Why did it happen to them?"

DEPRESSION: The loss becomes more conscious, sadness emerges. There's a reluctance for comforting company, and uncertainty and fear about the future and decisions arise.

ACCEPTANCE: A reflective process begins regarding the loss, attempting to find some meaning in it.

LEARNING: Hints of building a new reality start to appear. The loss is shared with others, and consolation is offered to others.

These stages can be applicable to children's grieving experiences as well, though they might manifest differently due to their age, level of comprehension, and emotional development.

However, depending on the age and developmental stage, children's reactions can vary. Let's take the case of a close loss in children between 6 and 9 years old:

- **Denial:** Denial serves as a defensive barrier to prevent emotional impact. Their reaction might involve aggression or, conversely, being happier and more playful than usual.

- **Idealization:** Insisting on idealizing the deceased person. This allows them to maintain an imaginary relationship and distance themselves from the pain.

- **Guilt**: Due to limited vocabulary and an inability to express themselves verbally, they may recall phrases from the deceased person's life.

- **Fear:** It's normal for children at this age to have fears about different things and situations, which can make them feel scared and vulnerable. They might hide their feelings, especially because they don't want their peers to see them as "different."

They might fear being left alone.

- **Taking care of others:** If the loss is of a close family member, they might take on the role of that person.

These reactions are influenced by their age, cognitive development, and emotional maturity. It's important for caregivers to provide a supportive and understanding environment, allowing children to express their emotions and providing comfort during their grieving process.

We can also add, and it's not a minor detail, that irritability and moodiness are common reactions. Due to this, adults often scold or reprimand them, which can lead to the children becoming aggressive as a defense mechanism. There's also a decrease in motivation for usual enjoyable activities and a dissatisfaction with their surroundings.

Among the changes in behavior, we can find:

- Loss of appetite.

- Appearance of physical pains such as headaches, stomachaches, etc., which can be somatizations or invented as a way to demand attention.

- Heightened sensitivity.

- Lack of energy and enthusiasm.

- Regression to earlier stages, such as thumb-sucking.

- Resurgence of bedwetting.

- Increased fear of the dark.

- Fear of being alone.

- Anxiety about being alone at bedtime.

- Refusal to go to school.

- Decrease in school performance.

These behavioral changes are responses to grief and can be quite normal in children who are coping with loss. It's essential for caregivers to be patient, empathetic, and understanding during this challenging time, offering support and communication to help them process their emotions.

How to deliver news of a death?

One of the toughest moments in life is having to communicate a death to a child. If we're obligated to do so, it's because the deceased person is close or known to the child.

First and foremost, it's best if the news is delivered by the child's parents, a family member, or someone emotionally close. The news should be shared calmly, not dramatically, with clear and simple words, allowing the child to ask any questions they feel necessary.

Choose a quiet place to communicate the news, free from distractions, to avoid confusion and misunderstandings. This is the moment to provide reassurance that you will be there unconditionally for whatever they need, while also clarifying that what happened to the person doesn't have to happen to them. Deliver the news as soon as possible to prevent them from finding out through another source, which could create a difficult-to-manage situation.

The manner in which you share the news is crucial: always tell the truth. A saying goes, *"lies have short legs"* and in these matters, lying to the child will undermine your credibility and leave them to their imagination.

Be as brief as possible. Giving excessive details is not advisable, as depending on the child's age, you might use words they don't understand or unnecessarily scare them. For example, avoid saying things like *"they're placed in a box and then in a three-meter hole in the ground, covered with lots of dirt"* and certainly avoid any mention of *"put in an oven and burned to ashes that are then scattered or kept"*. The information should always be tailored to the child's knowledge and developmental stage..

I want to emphasize that the person who died will no longer be with us physically but can remain close through our memories. Highlight that, even though they won't come back, they'll always be in our memories. Explain that there won't be any contact with the deceased person anymore.

How to help children cope with loss?

It's important to help children understand and make sense of their emotions. There are small actions we can take during or after a loss. The presence of an adult is crucial. The child should not be alone or feel alone, as it would increase their distress. Initially, it might be difficult for the parent, who also needs to process the loss, but spending time with the child is extremely important so they can ask any necessary questions. It's positive that they ask questions because it shows that they are not internalizing everything, but rather they are open to the situation, and it gives us an opportunity to understand their feelings and provide help.

The child will handle the loss in a less aggressive way in a safe, warm, and affectionate environment, with people they trust. Therefore, it's necessary for them to feel the presence of the adult, encouraging them to express their emotions and feelings without feeling pressured. Sometimes, the adult's own anxiety might lead them to ask too many questions, so it's important to wisely choose who will deliver the news to the child.

One of the best ways to reach the child's feelings is by asking questions like: *"What do you think about this?" "How does it seem to you?" "How are you feeling now?"*

It's expected that expressing emotions, ideas, and fears verbally might be difficult for a young child. To address this, we can use strategies such as hands-on activities, drawing, or using toys to represent their feelings. We will discuss some practical suggestions for this later.

Posture is crucial; sitting on the floor next to the child and away from noise will create a sense of trust and remove the feeling of being interrogated. Contact should flow naturally.

But what about rituals? Often, to protect the child, they are kept away from family activities such as wakes, funerals, or memorials. However, if the child chooses to attend these activities, it can facilitate the process of accepting the loss. Of course, one should always be attentive to the child's reaction, as their expectations might clash with reality and be detrimental. If they seem tense or sad (perhaps influenced by the overall somber atmosphere), it might be necessary to remove them so they can process their feelings on their own. This depends on their age and the nature of the context.

And then what? Afterward, there's emptiness, questions, and fears. This is when adults, alongside their own process of grieving, should be willing to let the child express how they're feeling. As we discussed earlier, this might manifest through reactions, tantrums, academic struggles, insomnia, and so on. It's important to spend more time with them, according to their age: playing, reading, letting them choose a story, cooking, or any other activity that opens the door to their emotions and, above all, makes them feel accompanied.

Certainly, there can be complications in a child's grieving process, especially when the loss is of someone close. Certain behaviors are expected during the grieving process, and when we talk about complications, we refer to variations in intensity and duration. While the grieving process is unique for each individual, it might be more intense in terms of feelings and prolonged in terms of duration for a child. That's why it's crucial to be attentive to any manifestation, whether it's expressed outwardly or, conversely, if the child becomes withdrawn (not talking, not eating, not laughing, and not wanting to play). Children often mirror the attitudes of their parents or caregivers.

The child's environment, including places like school (kindergarten, primary school), sports clubs, or religious institutions, should be informed about the loss. This helps provide support and containment, as these are places where the child might express their frustration, anger, or any other pent-up emotions.

Now, while we've focused on grief in the context of death, let's remember that grief can also arise from any type of separation that affects a child, disconnecting them from a person or object with whom they've formed an emotional bond and feel a sense of security. Therefore, we shouldn't overlook other types of losses, such as a miscarriage experienced by the child's mother, which may involve the loss of a long-awaited sibling, or situations like moving or parental separation. Although these events are experienced as forms of grief, they have notable differences. In the case of a miscarriage experienced by the child's mother while the child is anticipating a new sibling, the unborn sibling is already a part of the family's universe. Setting up a crib, decorating a room, buying clothes, and even referring to the baby by name all contribute to the unborn child's presence in the family. Depending on the child's age, if they are very young, they may not fully comprehend what happened. They will sense the sadness in the household, hear their parents' tears, but they might not necessarily grieve, as they didn't see their sibling (they might perceive the moment as the death of dreams and expectations). However, if the child is older, they may indeed experience pain and grief.

The way to communicate the news should follow the same principles we've discussed earlier: Explain it using simple words and brief sentences, avoid lengthy explanations or ambiguous words that are difficult to understand, have a trusted person with an emotional bond convey the news, and ensure it happens in a peaceful setting, allowing space for the child to express their emotions.

In the case of a planned move, technology can be a valuable tool to help the child adjust. You can show them beautiful places in the new area, present the move as a family adventure where they can discover new friends and climates. Turning the process of packing their clothes and toys into a game, organizing them by size or colors, can make the transition more engaging and less daunting. Of course, it's important to explain to them what will happen and to avoid lying. Often, adults have greater anxieties about such changes than children, who often approach these situations with more natural acceptance.

Within the emotional and imaginative capabilities of the adult caring for the child, it's beneficial to engage in activities together, ideally as a family. This not only allows the child to channel their emotions but also to perceive the familial atmosphere and the comfort they receive. Among these activities, you can use emotion lists that are readily available online. Such lists can help the child identify and articulate their feelings through play. For example, the child might use the word "sad" to describe all negative emotions, whether it's pain, distress, or sorrow, due to the limited vocabulary of young children. However, for school-aged children and those around 8 or 9 years old, this exercise can be particularly useful.

There are published books and stories designed to assist in the process of grieving. These stories can be read to children to help them feel less alone and to show them how others have dealt with their pain. If the child is able to read and write, you might suggest writing a letter to the departed loved one, to the town they had to move from, or even to that sibling they never got to meet. For younger children, providing a blank notebook for them to draw in freely can be helpful. They might draw situations they remember, pleasant moments, or even the sad ones.

Seeking help from a professional should not be seen as a last resort. It's better to have the support of a psychologist, grief counselor, child thanatologist, or educational psychologist during the grieving process, rather than addressing crises that could arise later from unresolved grief. Similarly, it's never too late to accompany the child through their grief process.

This brings us to the question of what to do if you know that a person close to the child is going to die. This situation might arise due to serious illnesses, terminal illnesses, or in the event of a serious accident. When faced with the news of a tragedy or severe illness, the adult or family unit might wonder whether it's best to inform the child. The benefit of communicating such news is, first and foremost, preventive. Children are highly attuned to the emotions of their environment, and they can easily sense when something is amiss. This perception of a distressing environment might lead them to create their own explanations for what's happening (thinking they misbehaved or are somehow responsible), leading to feelings of frustration and fear.

On the other hand, children decode conversations both verbal and nonverbal, tones, and evasiveness. By explaining to them what is happening (always in accordance with their age and providing only necessary information), we are taking into account their emotional needs, which are crucial for family relationships and trust.

It's often advised that when talking to children about, for example, a loved one's cancer, one should avoid using the word "cancer." Instead, you might explain that the body is affected and that they will undergo a treatment that will help but might also make them tired (to differentiate between the symptoms of the illness and the effects of chemotherapy), as they could think that the treatment itself is causing their loved one's condition.

Maintaining their routine is extremely important, including birthdays, sports, and other activities. Throughout life, we all experience losses; we don't all experience them the same way or with the same intensity. But losing something or someone reminds us of our finiteness and encourages us to value each moment and each connection as unique. And that's the legacy we should aim to pass on to our children.

Chapter 4

"MENTAL AND BEHAVIORAL PROBLEMS"

Cintia Puleo – Ana Kelleyian

Child and Adolescent Psychiatry is a subspecialty of psychiatry, which itself is a medical specialty. More than any other, psychiatry aims to equally address the mind and body. Its scope encompasses the cognitive, emotional, interpersonal, and behavioral processes of the patient, while navigating family, social, cultural, economic, religious, educational, and political contexts. Child psychiatry focuses on individuals ranging from childhood to adolescence, and many practitioners extend their care into young adulthood.

Disorders are not diagnosed based on isolated actions. That's why the duration of persistent behavior is taken into consideration.

The child and their development

The development of the child involves growth and maturation in various spheres, including the physical, cognitive, emotional, behavioral, and situational judgment abilities. As children have not yet reached adult capacity in these areas, they require the protection and care of caregivers. In general, parents fulfill this role, but in other cases, family members, government agencies, or other designated individuals provide the environments for children to mature.

Normal development can only be understood within the context and culture in which it occurs, which can either promote or hinder it. It's important to note that, except for early mental or physical disorders, developmental gaps and deviations from the norm at different times are not necessarily predictive of later developmental deficits or delays. Traits or abilities can be modified throughout life, although they are generally more malleable in early development. This notion of plasticity is an important characteristic of normal child development.

Neurodevelopment is the process by which the nervous system - and the brain as its main organ - grows, matures, and acquires its functions. It begins during gestation and continues into adulthood. It's a phenomenon that occurs on a continuum. At all times, multiple processes and skill acquisitions occur simultaneously, which also influence each other to advance the functional capacity of the nervous system.

The observation of nervous system development can be simplified into four stages:

1. **Anatomical Stage:** Occurs during gestation. The basic structure of the brain forms, involving three relevant processes: genesis, maturation, and grouping of nerve cells to form various organs of the nervous system.

2. **Motor Stage:** Occurs from birth to three years old. Learning postural and motor control takes place, enabling three major human characteristics: bipedalism, manual dexterity, and speech.

3. **Language and Environmental Understanding Stage:** Alongside the development of speech, basic language learning becomes integrated into brain circuits. From three years old to adolescence, the child's main focus is understanding the environment and developing abstract thinking, which relies on language.

4. **Personal Identity Stage:** Begins in adolescence and continues into adulthood. The foundational circuits acquired during the motor stage enrich with cultural learning. These circuits become refined and specialized as the adolescent decides which skills to develop, leading to becoming an independent adult.

In each of these stages, mental processes are guided and limited by emerging circuits, resulting in different qualities of thinking capacity and intelligence in each stage.

The normal and the pathological

A neurodevelopmental disorder is a deviation from the expected development for a certain age, linked to the formation of brain circuits. These disorders begin in childhood, but their expression varies at each stage as the central nervous system develops. It's common for several disorders to coincide in the same individual, making it challenging to differentiate one from another. The causes can be genetic or environmental, occurring during gestation, the neonatal period, or early childhood. These causes should be identified as early as possible to expose the child to experiences that are most suitable for their individual capabilities, aiming to help the altered circuits reach their maximum developmental potential. The longer they go without attention, the less likely it is to influence the growth of these abnormal circuits and the more difficult it becomes to improve their prognosis.

Stages of evaluating the psychological state in children and adolescents:

1.   **Interview with parents/guardians:** This provides an initial understanding of the child's symptoms and environment. The child's school performance and other activities are taken into account.

2.   **Examination of the child's mental state:** This involves an objective description, not interpretation, of the child's appearance, symptoms, behavior, and functioning observed during the interview. It can be conducted while the child engages in play or drawing (for younger children) or through directed interviews for older children.

3.   **Medical history and physical examination:** These are fundamental to rule out organic pathology causing the psychopathological symptoms and guide treatment. Additionally, evaluating the patient's health before the consultation is important for medication recommendations.

Principal psychopathological diagnoses:

Mental disorders can be classified based on their cause as organic or functional. Organic disorders are those resulting from an underlying medical condition that should be treated initially. Functional disorders do not offer concrete indications of physical alterations. This classification is highly important as it guides treatment approaches.

Neurodevelopmental Disorders

1. Intellectual Disabilities

Intellectual disability or intellectual developmental disorder is characterized by a deficit in the child's overall functioning and adaptability, beginning during the developmental period.

Global developmental delay involves a deficit in the expected milestones of intellectual development. Diagnosis is made in children under 5 years of age when the clinical severity level cannot be reliably assessed during childhood.

Unspecified intellectual disability is a diagnosis reserved for individuals over 5 years of age when the degree of intellectual disability is challenging to evaluate due to sensory, physical deficits, severe behaviors, or comorbidity with a mental disorder.

2. Communication Disorders

Language disorder is characterized by difficulties in acquiring and using language across different modalities due to deficits in comprehension or production.

Speech sound disorders involve difficulties in producing sounds that interfere with comprehension or hinder verbal communication messages.

Childhood-onset fluency disorder or stuttering is an alteration in speech fluency and pattern, inappropriate for the individual's age and language skills, persisting over time.

Social communication disorder or pragmatic disorder is characterized by difficulties in using verbal and nonverbal communication, leading to limitations in social relationships or academic performance.

3. Autism Spectrum Disorder (ASD)

ASD is a neurodevelopmental disorder primarily characterized by significant, persistent deficits in social communication and interaction across multiple contexts, accompanied by patterns of restricted and repetitive behavior, interests, and activities. It may or may not be accompanied by intellectual disability.

4. Deficit Attention Hyperactivity Disorder (or ADD, ADHD)

It is determined by the presence of a persistent pattern of inattention and/or hyperactivity-impulsivity that interferes with development. It can present with a predominance of hyperactivity or combined with lack of attention.

5. Specific Learning Disorder

Academic skills are quantifiably below the individual's chronological age, causing interference in daily life activities. It can be classified with difficulty in reading, written expression, or mathematics.

6. Motor Disorders

This diagnosis includes both disorders due to deficit of skills and those caused by the presence of inappropriate motor habits.

Developmental Coordination Disorder. Difficulties manifest as clumsiness, slowness, and lack of precision in performing motor skills that interfere with daily life activities.

Stereotyped Movement Disorder. Characterized by repetitive, impulsive, and non-purposeful motor behavior, similar to a choreography (chorea). Self-injurious behavior may be present.

Tic Disorders. A tic is a sudden, rapid, recurrent, and non-rhythmic movement or vocalization. It is a transient tic disorder if the tics have been present for less than a year since their onset.

Tourette's Disorder. Defined by multiple motor tics and one or more vocal tics that have persisted for more than a year since their onset. Its onset is prior to 18 years of age.

Schizophrenia and Other Psychotic Disorders Spectrum

They can be classified as:

Brief Psychotic Disorder. Characterized by one or more psychotic symptoms (delusions, hallucinations, disorganized speech, catatonic or disorganized behavior, negative symptoms) that manifest between one day and one month, after which the person may return to their premorbid level of functioning. The symptoms cannot be due to another illness or substance use.

Schizophrenia. A serious illness characterized by a loss of reality judgment and the presence of positive symptoms (hallucinations, delusions, disorganized behavior, etc.) and negative symptoms (apathy, abulia, affective flattening, etc.) to varying degrees, leading to cognitive deterioration. In younger children, not all psychopathological symptoms can be present due to their cognitive immaturity. For example, disorders of thought process can be seen from around 7 years of age.

Other less common classifications. Here are Medication-Induced Psychotic Disorder, Psychotic Disorder Due to Medical Conditions, and Catatonia.

Mood Disorders

Depression. Based on the presence of persistent widespread feelings of sadness and unhappiness, loss of capacity to enjoy daily activities, and irritability associated with other symptoms.

Bipolar Disorder. This diagnosis can involve manic, hypomanic, and depressive episodes. A manic episode is characterized by feelings of grandiosity or increased self-esteem; decreased need for sleep, being more talkative than usual, subjective experience that thoughts are racing, easy distractibility, increased goal-directed activity (social, occupational, school, or sexual) or psychomotor agitation (activity not goal-directed).

Anxiety Disorders

Separation Anxiety Disorder. Characterized by intense fear or anxiety related to the prospect of separating from a person with whom a close bond is formed. Present for at least 4 weeks.

Selective Mutism. Persistent inability to speak or respond to others in a specific social situation despite speaking comfortably in other situations. Present for at least one month.

Specific Phobia. Intense or persistent fear or anxiety about a specific object or situation, such as animals, environments, blood, injections, etc. Present for at least six months.

Social Anxiety Disorder. Intense fear or anxiety that appears in relation to one or more social situations in which the person is exposed. Present for at least six months.

Panic Disorder. Characterized by unexpected or recurrent panic attacks, followed by persistent apprehension or worry about the onset of new attacks and their consequences.

Generalized Anxiety Disorder. Defined by excessive and persistent fear and worry about various events or activities associated with physiological hyperarousal.

Obsessive-Compulsive Disorder and Related Disorders

Obsessive-Compulsive Disorder. The essential feature of this diagnosis is the presence of recurrent obsessions or compulsive acts. The former are intrusive ideas, images, or mental impulses that repeatedly intrude upon the individual's mental activity. They are usually distressing and the individual experiencing them typically tries, often unsuccessfully, to resist them. They are perceived as one's own thoughts, despite being involuntary and often repulsive. In contrast, compulsive acts or rituals are behaviors that are repeated over and over again. They are not inherently pleasurable nor do they give rise to useful activities in themselves. For the person, they function to prevent some objectively unlikely event.

Trichotillomania. Despite efforts to stop or reduce the symptoms, the individual recurrently pulls out their hair, causing distress. Hair loss occurs, but not due to any illness or medication.

Excoriation Disorder. Despite efforts to stop, the individual repeatedly damages their skin, causing distress due to social injury. The excoriation is not due to any illness, medication, or other mental disorders.

Onychophagia. Despite not wanting to, the person bites their nails, of hands and/or feet. The statistic in children under 10 years old is 30%, and in individuals with ADHD, it reaches 75%. Causes include imitation, low self-esteem, shyness, and nervousness. It can cause injuries and infections around the nails.

Trauma and Stress-Related Disorders

Reactive Attachment Disorder. Characterized by inappropriate and disturbed ways of relating in most social interactions. Symptoms may include: rejecting caregiver, avoiding physical contact, difficulty being comforted, failing to distinguish social interactions with strangers, preferring to be alone rather than interacting with others.

Post-Traumatic Stress Disorder (PTSD). Arising from exposure to death, serious injury, and/or sexual violence, whether real or threatened. Presence of one or more of the following symptoms: distressing or recurrent intrusive memories or dreams, dissociative reactions where the individual feels or acts as if the traumatic event were recurring, intense or prolonged psychological distress upon exposure to cues that symbolize or resemble an aspect of the traumatic event, and persistent avoidance of stimuli associated with the traumatic event.

Somatomorf Disorder

This involves the chronic and exhaustive seeking of medical help for multiple physical symptoms that do not correspond to any illness. The provocation can come from parents, grandparents, or other significant individuals.

Feeding Disorders

Pica. This refers to the persistent consumption of non-nutritive substances for a period of at least one month (e.g., dirt, paper, feces, etc.).

Avoidant/Restrictive Food Intake Disorder (ARFID):

Anorexia Nervosa: Characterized by energy intake restriction relative to requirements, leading to significantly low body weight in the context of age, sex, developmental trajectory, and physical health. Accompanied by intense fear of gaining weight or becoming fat and a disturbance in the way one's body weight or shape is experienced.

It can be classified into two types: "restrictive," where weight loss is primarily due to diet, fasting, and/or excessive exercise, or "binge/purge.".

Bulimia Nervosa: Defined by recurrent episodes of binge eating within a discrete period of time, associated with a sense of lack of control over eating during the episode and inappropriate compensatory behaviors to avoid weight gain, such as self-induced vomiting, misuse of laxatives, diuretics, or other medications, fasting, or excessive exercise.

Excretion Disorders

Enuresis. It is the repeated emission of urine during the day or night, involuntarily in bed or clothing, at least twice a week for a minimum of three consecutive months, in children aged 5 years or older.

Encopresis. It is a type of incontinence that consists of repeated evacuation of feces in inappropriate places, usually unintentionally and starting from the age of 4 years.

In both types of incontinence, they can be classified as primary in children who have never had an episode of incontinence for prolonged periods of time or secondary when there has been complete self-control for at least 6 months.

Sleep-Wake Disorders

Insomnia. According to the American Academy of Sleep Medicine, it is the "persistent difficulty with sleep initiation and/or sleep maintenance, along with the quality of the sleep that is adequate to the age and developmental stage of the individual." Prevalence is estimated between 1% and 6% in the general pediatric population, being higher in children with neurological developmental disorders or other chronic psychiatric or medical disorders. The diagnosis of behavioral insomnia of sleep onset depends on the presence of maladaptive and inappropriate associations with going to sleep, such as falling asleep while being rocked, watching television/screens, or in the parents' bed.

Parasomnias. These are unpleasant physical events or experiences that occur at sleep onset, during sleep, or upon awakening. These include sleepwalking, night terrors, nightmares, nocturnal enuresis, sleep-related groaning, etc.

Restless Sleep. It is characterized by excessive movements of some parts or the entire body.

Daytime Sleepiness. Presents persistent tiredness and lack of energy, with a tendency to nap during the day.

Night Terrors. Children are asleep, can sit up, walk, talk, and are difficult to calm during the episode, but they do not remember it afterward.

Nightmares. Unlike night terrors, children remember the details and since they are awake, they can be comforted and can communicate with others, albeit with limited speech and movement.

Impulse Control and Conduct Disorders

Oppositional Defiant Disorder. Characterized by uncooperative, defiant, negative, irritable, and angry behaviors toward parents, peers, teachers, and other authority figures.

Intermittent Explosive Disorder. Defined by recurrent behavioral outbursts manifested by verbal aggression (such as tantrums, verbal disputes, or fights) or physical aggression against property, animals, or other individuals, over a period of 3 months. The level of aggression expressed is significantly disproportionate to the triggering factor.

<u>Conduct Disorder.</u> Manifested through a repetitive and persistent pattern of behavior that violates the basic rights of others, as well as age-appropriate social norms or rules.

Substance-Related and Addictive Disorders

<u>Substance Use Disorders.</u> It is a chronic disorder that causes physiological, clinical, behavioral, and cognitive symptoms attributed to the use of alcohol and/or substances.

The DSM-5 (Diagnostic and Statistical Manual of Mental Disorders, the current international 5th edition) classifies psychoactive substances into 10 classes of drugs: alcohol, caffeine, cannabis, hallucinogens, inhalants, opioids, sedatives/hypnotics/anxiolytics, stimulants, tobacco, and other substances.

For diagnosis, two of the following criteria must be met for 12 months: hazardous use, social or interpersonal problems related to use, failure to fulfill major roles due to use, withdrawal syndrome (also for cannabis), tolerance, using larger amounts or for a longer time, repeated efforts to cut down or control use, spending more time than intended on substance-related activities, having physical or psychological problems related to use, giving up other activities due to use. It is classified into three levels of severity based on the number of criteria met: mild, moderate, and severe.

<u>Non-Substance-Related Addictive Disorders</u>. The so-called "behavioral addictions" are not chemically dependent on an external agent but on the interaction of recurrent reward with the addict's personality. Due to the selective behavioral repetition of the brain reward circuits and stress, similar to substance addiction, they can take over normal functioning and lead to addictions. Only Gambling Disorder is recognized. Other behavioral disorders such as food addiction (and its contribution to obesity) or addiction to internet games, cyberaddictions, among others, are not incorporated.

Neurocognitive Disorders

Delirium is an acute and often reversible alteration of mental status, characterized by symptom fluctuation, impaired attention, disorganized thinking, and altered alertness. It is associated with various illnesses and persistent cognitive deficits.

The concepts in this chapter are strict and measured, but they need to be to achieve a consensus-based professional diagnosis with similar characteristics worldwide. From this foundational text, variations of each disorder emerge based on personal psychological characteristics, context, customs, environment, culture, and others that each professional should observe and determine an appropriate and functional psychological/psychiatric treatment; sometimes personal, family, school, etc.

To those reading this chapter, we suggest: do not self-diagnose, it's better to consult a professional than to make assumptions or tell others they have a disorder. Be cautious.

Chapter 5

SEXUALITY AND GENDER

Yolanda Weigandt

Understanding the differences between "sexuality" and "gender" leads us to think of the human being as an integrated being, created with a body, soul, spirit, and a social nature.

Distinguishing between sexuality and genitalia is essential to eradicate prejudices and embrace diversity. While genitalia are a biologically determined and genetically transmitted condition, sexuality is something that is constructed throughout life: sexual relationships are just a part of it.

Sexuality

The term "sex" is used to classify human beings into two broad groups: male and female, and also refers to sexual practice.

In this way, sexuality becomes an expression that encompasses all knowledge, behavior, beliefs, attitudes, and values of the individual.

It encompasses dimensions related to the anatomy, psychology, and biochemistry of an individual's sexual response: their identity, orientation, functions, personality, as well as their thoughts, feelings, and relationships.

The World Health Organization (WHO) defines: *"Sexuality is a central aspect of being human, present throughout life. It encompasses sex, gender identities and roles, eroticism, pleasure, intimacy, reproduction, and sexual orientation."*.

"Sexuality" also refers to the set of relationships that individuals establish with each other and with the world, simply because they are sexual beings. It implies recognition as a person of a certain sex, with the capacity to give and receive love and pleasure.

We were created as men and women by God, intended to develop ourselves in all areas of our lives. Our way of being, feeling, enjoying, and transcending is related to our sexuality.

The brain is the primary sexual organ; if the brain becomes aroused, our genital organs will also respond. Therefore, we must understand that a healthy and proper sexuality begins in the brain, in our values, in our spirit, in our understanding, and in our mind.

Our psychosexuality develops under the same evolutionary process as our physical development. The relationship with parents and parental roles are fundamental pillars in the correct development of one's psychosexuality.

Gender

From conception to the age of seven, following certain patterns of maturation, there are learnings that will remain forever. That's why teaching about sexuality in incorrect, harmful, or ideological ways can either enhance or traumatize personality and behaviors for a lifetime. Sexes have hormonal, environmental, and genetic differences that promote different behaviors: each person is different, and massifying loses individual identity.

Regarding the self-perception of one's own sexuality, it can be stated that it is real. Each individual is what they self-perceive to be: based on self-esteem criteria, the desire for recognition, exaggeration, or histrionics. The difference lies in the social, cultural, and religious consensus in which a certain perception is shared.

From conception, chromosomes dictate the sex of the unborn baby: male or female. There is a genetic norm that marks the fetus as such. *The biological aspect prevails*, as stated by Dr. Ana Kelleyian in her book "Menos 9 a 18 guía para padres y maestros" (Minus 9 to 18 Guide for Parents and Teachers).

The differences between the female and male brain and their functions, as well as their physical and cognitive structures, have become specialized to ensure the future of the species. Gender changes are always forced (except for deformities) and underestimate one's intrinsic value. The female and male sexes are biologically, psychologically, and behaviorally complementary. Altering the biological aspect goes against nature for a lifetime.

Gender Ideology

Gender ideology consists of saying "you choose what you want to be"; man or woman. This concept aims to be culturally implanted. Every cell in my organism defines whether I am a "man or woman," and even thinking that I could modify this is a clear threat to human nature, the individual, and things.

Gender ideology has infiltrated schools, institutes, and textbooks. As parents, we must be cautious about the information children receive, paying attention to the teachings in the schools they attend. Remember that a child is like a sponge, absorbing everything they receive to later define their personality.

Upon entering care and educational institutions (ages 3, 4, 5), children primarily learn through play. The attempted teaching of sexuality education (ESI) with gender ideology from the age of two distorts the child's process of identification and differentiation.

Children can be introduced to doubting their sexuality, confusing their feelings, and mixing up situations of friendship with other types of situations. All of this leads to ambiguous emotional situations.

Every confusion leads to anxiety, anguish, and a loss of peace. A confused child or adolescent who doesn't know who or how they are, what they want, or what they need becomes an easy target to be led in any direction.

Through laws and governmental guidelines, there is an increasing tendency to disorient the human being. It's impossible to think that in the long run, this human being won't be destined for confusion of the mind and soul.

What is in crisis today is the human being, largely due to the implementation of gender ideology. Trying to implant in children, adolescents, and young people the concept/belief that they are sexually neutral beings is causing a misunderstanding and dichotomy between the mind and the body, between family and school, resulting in academic failure and dropouts. Educating children this way from a young age leads them to future confusion in forming relationships and taking responsible commitments towards a new generation.

LGTB+ Movement

The LGBT+ liberation movement (Lesbian, Gay, Bisexual, Transgender, and more), or movement for free sexual orientation, refers to a social movement in which the cause of individuals with a non-heterosexual sexual orientation is fought for. It is a culturally and politically driven movement that aims to deconstruct traditional masculinity and promote diverse and entirely malleable masculinity. This movement's purpose is to dehumanize and demoralize men. Everything is within the freedom to choose and embraces all kinds of degeneration, without limits and responsibility, promising freedom and diversity while destroying the individual and society.

Human beings absorbed in their desires and passions are establishing the guiding parameters of their own lives. Everything is called into question, even more so when it doesn't align with personal preferences. Nothing manages to be held as an unquestionable value, so that if a forty-year-old man wakes up one day and feels/perceives himself as an 8-year-old girl, it's okay! Is it within his right...? Who can deny it? Social condemnation, mental illness, exploitation of circumstances, become sustenance for those who want to be part of this movement and don't dare.

Generalization of minorities, promotion of small groups, we are all... we all have exclusive freedoms...

Increasingly, we see politics, culture, art, and religion saturated with this ideology, the same cultural indoctrination based on emotions and irrationality. It's important not to normalize it.

The possibility we face today of being able to choose, almost unquestioningly, what aligns best with our tastes and preferences, and the fact that personal choices are always valid because they're founded on one's own "truth," the multitude of factors that form the breeding ground where the reality we live in is gestated, allows this entire ideology to become an intrinsic part of the human being.

Homosexuality

The term homosexuality refers to exclusive sexual attraction toward individuals of the same sex. Men attracted to other men are commonly referred to as gay, while women attracted to other women are known as lesbians.

Homosexuality is not the linear outcome of a single factor, but rather a complex interplay of various factors: genes, family environment, faith, childhood experiences, and social events. These variables may have an influence, but they don't necessarily determine it.

All these areas play a relevant role in defining homosexuality. We cannot attribute it solely to one area. It's an intricate interaction of diverse factors and life experiences.

There is no scientific evidence to support the genetic theory of homosexuality or to demonstrate that it could be innate.

Therefore, we can say that homosexuality is a bio-psychosocial-spiritual experience in which a person feels an erotic impulse towards individuals of the same sex.

Homosexuality is not associated with physical-genital intimacy between individuals of the same sex, but with the feelings one has in response to the sexual, physical, social, or psychological attraction exerted by individuals of the same sex.

Homosexuality is a learned behavior in the psychosexual development during childhood and adolescence.

The relationship with parents and parental role are fundamental pillars in the proper psychosexual development. Often, the home environment is where a child identifies with the same-sex parental figure. This identification is crucial for the child's sexual development. The father (or a significant substitute figure) is the one who affirms the child in their role.

The term Bisexuality refers to sexual attraction toward individuals of both the same sex and the opposite sex, although not necessarily with the same frequency or intensity for each case.

When we refer to Transsexuality, we are talking about individuals who, despite having a certain biological sex, identify with the opposite sex. To adopt this way of life, they can take hormones or estrogen, gradually transforming the body until reaching gender reassignment surgery (if they choose to undergo it). Some individuals choose not to have surgery. This can occur in both men and women.

Pornography

Pornography refers to all material that depicts explicit sexual acts and aims to generate sexual arousal in the consumer. It can appeal to both visual and auditory stimulation.

Human beings, absorbed in their desires and passions, seeking immediate pleasure, unable to delay gratification, not accepting a "no" as an answer.

In this world of pornography, the dominant view is that of men and their fantasies. We face one of the most significant addictions.

In a society where individuals were not trained to confront, tolerate, and overcome frustration, where there is no authority establishing the boundaries of right and wrong, and where everything is highly sexualized, an ideal context is created for the world of pornography.

We've reached a point where limits are only theoretical because the real world seems to have none; child pornography is an example of this.

Child sexual exploitation has multiple manifestations; it is a grave violation of the rights of children and adolescents, their sexual integrity, and their normal development. It inflicts both physical and emotional damage during a crucial developmental phase, with potential long-term consequences, stemming from the abuse itself and the continued circulation of underage individuals' images on the internet.

In Argentina, my country of residence, it is a crime to finance, offer, trade, publish, facilitate, disseminate, or distribute images of minors engaged in sexual activities or depicting their genitals for sexual purposes.

According to a 2023 statistic from the NGO Save the Children Spain, 7 out of 10 adolescents, or 68.2%, frequently consume pornographic content. The vast majority do so through their mobile phones, primarily focusing on free online content. The study found that teenagers first view pornography at the age of twelve and do so frequently. This consumption is mostly done in privacy, through mobile phones, and often involves content featuring violence and inequality.

With the advancement and progress of the internet, social media, and new technologies, "grooming" has become a method of harassment through online platforms. In this scenario, an adult (digital predator) creates a fake profile (posing as someone the victim's age), establishes a trusting connection, builds a friendship with the minor, and exerts emotional control through manipulation, deception, and even blackmail, with the goal of obtaining sexually explicit material from the minor and ultimately abusing them.

In my recommendation to parents, I suggest accompanying their children's device usage, discussing sexuality while respecting their developmental stage, talking about their online activities and content consumption, and setting rules while explaining the risks.

We firmly believe that living in purity is not a utopia; we believe it is possible and essential.

Stages of Psychosocial Development

Let's return to the basics where we explain what is considered normal, what is expected according to age, and the evolution of a child through various stages until reaching adulthood.

In his theory, Sigmund Freud developed the idea that sexual experiences are of great importance for the development of the human psyche. He mentioned that humans are born with a sex, and sexuality is not understood by him solely as adult sexual practices related to intercourse. In his theory of psychosocial development, he proposed the existence of five stages that each individual goes through: oral stage, anal stage, phallic stage, latency stage, and genital stage.

The Psychosocial Development theory put forth by Erik Erikson reinterprets the psychosocial stages developed by Freud, emphasizing the social aspects of each stage.

For the explanation of development, we also consider the contributions of Jean Piaget and his cognitive theory. According to Piaget, cognitive development is a continuous construction of the human being marked by various stages, needs, and actions.

Understanding a child's psychosocial development allows us to grasp the difficulties and problems a child must resolve at each stage to form their psyche. To comprehend this development and the changes that need to be navigated, we will evaluate the different stages.

Stage: Infancy (first two years of life)

This period is characterized by the child's complete dependence on their caregivers, requiring them for the satisfaction of their basic needs.

If the child's needs are met with minimal frustration, an affective sense of security will develop. This is expressed through breastfeeding, caresses, voice, and gazes. Repeating this experience gradually generates an internal representation in the infant that their caregivers are there to comfort them, establishing a secure bond with them and forming a sense of security.

If their needs are systematically unmet, the infant develops feelings of insecurity, incorporating a mental representation of the world as a hostile place, leading to a higher likelihood of forming an insecure attachment (ambivalent, avoidant, or disorganized).

In this period, which spans from birth to 12 to 18 months, the stage is characterized by trust or mistrust. The sense of whether it is possible to trust the world or not develops.

From a cognitive perspective, this developmental stage is characterized by sensorimotor intelligence, where intellectual development is closely tied to the actions a child takes in their environment. Learning occurs through the senses and motor activities.

Regarding psychosocial development, the stage that spans from birth to 12 to 18 months is the oral stage, during which the primary source of pleasure comes from activities involving the mouth. This explains the tendency of young children to want to "put everything in their mouths."

Stage: Early Childhood (2 to 5 years)

This stage is characterized by significant biological changes of a maturation nature that enable walking, sphincter control, and the emergence of symbolic function, along with language.

The child frequently opposes authority's commands with stubbornness and obstinacy as a way to assert themselves in front of others. This is why this stage is also referred to as the "age of obstinacy." This situation indicates that the child is discovering and developing their own identity.

Play appears in a child's life as a way to practice the recently acquired symbolic function. Through play, they take on roles and scenarios. Initially engaging in individualistic symbolic play, the child gradually transitions to collective play, where they need to interact with other children to achieve their goals. This collective symbolic play imitates adult behaviors, promoting the adaptation to gender roles they will later have in relation to their gender.

At this stage of development, curiosity about sexuality emerges. With a gradual exploration of their own bodies, children begin to understand themselves, leading to common games like "mom and dad" and "doctor and nurse." Exploring their genitals brings about pleasurable sensations, which can lead to behaviors like self-stimulation or childhood masturbation. These behaviors might be accompanied by feelings of fear or inhibition, greatly influenced by adults' reactions. Open dialogue and guidance with care are important. Explaining the concept of external genitals as "private" body parts can be helpful."

Children's thinking is egocentric, magical, and concrete, which should be taken into account when they ask questions about sexuality.

From 18 months to 3 years is the stage of autonomy and shame or doubt, developing a balance of independence. The child attempts to fulfill their desires. From ages 3 to 6, the stage of initiative develops as the child tries new things and isn't discouraged by failure.

Cognitively, the expected development between ages 2 and 7 transitions to representational intelligence, characterized by preoperational or symbolic thinking. Words are used to represent people, places, and events.

During the anal stage (up to age 3), the child focuses on sphincter control, experiencing pleasure in accumulation, retention, and expulsion. This grants them more control and the ability to assert their will, thus self-affirming. Between ages 3 and 6 is the phallic stage, where the genital region becomes the source of gratification.

Moral development at this stage relates to obedience to avoid punishment or gain advantage.

Intermediate Childhood Stage (From 6 Years to Puberty)

During this stage, a period of formal education and learning begins in school. The child needs to feel integrated within peer groups. Friendships between children of the same sex are common, reinforcing gender roles.

According to Erikson, this is the stage where the child must learn cultural skills or face feelings of inferiority. Through play, children start experiencing competition. It's a stage of intense intellectual work where the child constantly tests themselves and achieves results through their actions in the world.

Many changes occur in children from ages 7 to 12. There's a shift in thinking from intuitive to organizing concrete operations. This new way of thinking allows them to establish causal relationships, combining experiences with a more individual and critical view of the world around them.

During this period known as "latency," there's a seemingly calm phase compared to others. However, sexual curiosity, genital exploration, and childhood masturbation still exist, generally without eroticism.

Moral development during this stage is termed conventional, where the right thing is done to please others or obey the law.

Late Childhood to Adolescence Stage

This stage is biologically defined by the onset of puberty, marked by biological changes evidenced through the appearance of secondary sexual characteristics that lead to new ways of thinking, feeling, and behaving in relation to oneself and others for the child-adolescent.

Girls experience menarche (first menstruation), while boys commonly have nocturnal emissions (erections). This is due to the body producing more testosterone and, with it, sperm.

Masturbation is frequent during this stage and serves the purpose of aiding in self-knowledge of the body as well as releasing sexual tension. This occurs in both males and females.

The stage that begins with puberty is referred to as genital stage. With these biological changes, the body is prepared for reproduction.

Cognitive egocentrism is present, where adolescents see the world and interpersonal relationships from their own perspective. Simultaneously, they feel they're the center of attention for others, a phenomenon known as the "imaginary audience" or "imaginary spectators."

Another described phenomenon is the "personal fable," where adolescents feel invulnerable and consider themselves to be special beings. Additionally, they have a need to intellectualize and fantasize, along with a social rebellious attitude, critiquing and challenging societal norms.

This period is where adolescents often feel the most social pressure. It's natural during this phase to want to be liked by others, with a strong desire for group belonging.

Fluctuations in mood are common; however, persistent depression, suicidal ideation, self-harm, sleep disturbances, and prolonged discouragement should raise suspicions of potential mood disorders.

From puberty to early adulthood is the stage of identity or identity confusion, where adolescents must determine their own sense of self.

From around 12 years to adulthood, the stage of formal operations occurs, where individuals can think in abstract terms and confront hypothetical situations. It's also referred to as hypothetical-deductive thinking.

This stage is expected to foster an autonomous moral conscience, choosing values and moral principles that transcend group influences.

Young Adulthood Stage

The young adulthood stage of human development occurs after adolescence and before full adulthood, typically spanning from 18 to 25 years of age. It's characterized by personal development and economic independence.

Physically, their bodies have reached sexual maturity, and they are fully capable of reproduction. They have generally reached about 95% of their adult height and weight.

During this stage, young individuals often feel more at ease with themselves compared to their adolescent years, although they haven't yet reached the equilibrium characteristic of full adulthood. It's a prime time for learning, as reason and the ability to think have tempered the excesses of fantasy, allowing them to perceive reality as it is.

Many are still pursuing their education while also beginning to search for employment. There's a simultaneous need to separate from and depend on their parents. They seek to establish their own lifestyle.

Relationships with family tend to improve during this stage, and conflicts between parents and children usually decrease. Young adults may continue to question certain boundaries such as money, household chores, curfew, and appearance. This phase is generally more stable.

Some young adults begin to contemplate moving out and becoming independent. They take on new, more responsible roles. During this period, emotional dependence on parents diminishes, and commitment to romantic relationships progressively increases.

Individuals start to establish themselves in the workforce and are in the midst of professional development. It's a time of career growth and advancement.

In conclusion, the characteristics people are born with and the effects of their life experiences mutually influence one another, shaping development, which is a lifelong process.

Abnormal Sexual Behaviors

Abnormal sexual behaviors should be a cause for concern and

mental health evaluation. These behaviors include:

* Sexual behaviors not appropriate for the age: Behaviors that raise suspicion of sexual abuse, such as drawing or simulating sexual acts, asking others to touch their genitals, etc.

* Compulsive masturbation: When masturbation becomes the sole or primary source of satisfaction or tension relief, leading to social withdrawal or occurring in public.

* Persistent dissatisfaction with assigned sex or gender role: Assuming mannerisms and behaviors traditionally associated with the opposite gender, showing discomfort with the assigned sex or role.

It's important to address these behaviors promptly and seek professional help if necessary to ensure the individual's well-being and mental health.

Child Abuse Prevention

I will provide some advice on what to discuss with children from a young age to alert them to danger:

- Sexual organs are private parts of our bodies; no one can touch them or ask us to touch the private parts of others. That is not okay.

- If something an adult does makes them uncomfortable, they should move away and talk about what's bothering them.

- Teach them about "good" touches and "bad" touches.

- Teach them to say "No" in situations that make them uncomfortable.

- Keeping secrets about their bodies is not okay.

- Don't let strangers take photos of them.

- Help them share things that happen to them without fear, assuring them we will help.

When a child speaks about abuse, it's important to believe them. A young child between the ages of two and five finds it difficult to invent stories about abuse.

There are physical and behavioral symptoms that can lead us to suspect abuse, such as urinary tract infections, itching or pain in the genitals, torn or stained underwear, difficulty walking or sitting. We can also observe changes in eating habits, sleep disturbances (nightmares, insomnia), excessive fear or shyness around adults, difficulty concentrating, bedwetting, shame about their own body. These are some indicators. It's important to note that if a child has any of these symptoms, it's a clear sign of abuse, so it's important to investigate and seek help from the appropriate professional: a pediatrician or psychoanalyst.

Sex Education

Despite our own experiences and teachings on the subject, it's our responsibility as parents to provide age-appropriate sex education to our children.

Sex education is part of a series of explanations and answers that children seek about life.

During Childhood

During early childhood (2 to 5 years), as parents, we should address the topic of sexuality with normalcy and without fear, as children learn and discover themselves in the absolute trust of their parents.

From the age of two, children become curious about the differences in sex.

The best way to answer these questions is to teach them about anatomical differences, discussing parts of the human body: head, arms, legs, genital organs, always using their correct names (penis, vagina, vulva). We should always use accurate terms. To help with this, we can use educational books that address the topic according to their age.

Between the ages of four and five, children might ask how babies are born, either because their mother is pregnant or when they see someone on the street and become curious.

Parents often feel anxious about their children's questions; just answer the question. Many times, the child only expects a simple response. We can tell them that the baby is warm and growing in the mommy's tummy, and when the time comes, the baby will be with us.

If the question is about how the baby comes out, explain naturally that the baby comes out through the vagina, which stretches to allow the baby to pass.

If they ask how the baby got into the tummy, it's recommended to avoid using fictional stories, but you can use analogies: "Daddy has a tiny seed, and mommy has another tiny seed. When these come together, a baby starts forming in mommy's tummy. After 9 months, mommy will bring the baby into the world through childbirth." The important thing is always to tell the truth, answer clearly and simply.

It's not necessary to give too much information; as they mature, they will continue to ask questions. If a child attends preschool, it's advisable to discuss how the topic will be approached with the teacher. Let's not forget that it's our responsibility as parents to provide sex education to our children.

If children don't ask, don't worry; not all children are the same. As parents, we can inquire about their level of understanding and then discuss the topic accordingly.

From a very young age, we should teach children about their sexual organs. These parts are not dirty or ugly; they're private parts of our body, and we should take care of them. When we use the bathroom, we should close the door. It's not advisable for parents to shower naked with their children; they can wear swimsuits. This way, we teach them about preserving their privacy.

Regarding conception and sexual intercourse, it's advisable to wait until the child is around seven or eight years old, allowing them to mature before discussing this topic with them.

As parents, we must select and monitor what children watch and listen to, as there is currently a vast amount of explicit sexual information and images accessible to them. This can potentially harm their psychoemotional development, as they are not prepared to receive certain information. We must supervise and protect our children from what they see and hear.

An important topic to consider is how to prevent child abuse, and this is a responsibility that falls on us as parents. Not providing proper information about sexuality leaves children vulnerable and exposed.

Statistics show that a high percentage of individuals who sexually abuse minors are from the child's close circle of family and acquaintances (neighbors, teachers, close relatives, and even the biological father of the child). These are people who are trusted and likable, making it difficult to suspect them. This is where the problem lies. While the majority are men, there are also female abusers.

Since we cannot truly know the intentions of the people who interact with our growing children, it's best to warn them. Therefore, remember this phrase: "An informed child is an empowered child: empowered to defend themselves."

Our behavior and the messages we convey through it are what teach the most during this stage. If as parents, we give lectures about sexuality while displaying suffering, distrust, and fear towards loved ones, the child will learn to distrust and perceive affectionate relationships with loved ones as unpleasant.

Demonstrations of affection (hugs, kisses, caresses) between parents are of vital importance for a child's learning and psychosexual development. Similarly, abuse, violence (both physical and verbal), degrade a healthy sexual education.

Parents are the most significant examples that children have when it comes to learning. At this age, children will ask out of curiosity, not because they are experiencing sexual needs. Remember that they are in the stage of "sexual latency," with substantial intellectual learning. Children in this stage have well-developed fantasies, so we should not leave them uninformed, as they might receive unhealthy information from other sources.

Let's not forget the fundamental principle of always telling the truth. If we don't know how to explain something to them, we can say, "I'll find out and we'll talk about this topic again." They accept the truth as something natural.

Children who have become accustomed to talking about sex openly with their parents and have received answers to their questions usually do not feel the need to seek out other types of information.

If an eight-year-old child hasn't asked how babies are born, it's advisable for parents to inquire about what information they already possess and clarify any doubts they might have.

Starting around the age of ten, we can explain to them that both men and women were not created to be sexual objects and that sex without love is not advisable.

It might seem innocent to ask children of this age if they have a boyfriend or girlfriend, teasing them or making inappropriate comments. However, at this stage, there isn't a sexual interest in the opposite sex. Let's avoid stimulating this and allow them to develop such interests naturally later on.

Many parents hesitate to talk about abuse with their children, fearing they might instill fear or make them overly suspicious of everyone. This is not the case. If we do discuss it, children will become more aware, and we can potentially save them from the hands of malicious individuals who could harm them.

An informed, attentive child with strong self-esteem is less likely to be a target for an abuser. Generally, sexual predators seek out vulnerable, uninformed children who have little communication with their parents.

In Adolescence

Let's learn to break the ice and establish conversations based on respect, love, and care.

During this stage, it's not about giving a lecture on sexuality; rather, the most important thing is to create a space and an atmosphere to be able to talk with our teenage children about anything. As parents, we should respect and acknowledge their opinions and interests, creating an environment of trust that allows for sincere and spontaneous dialogue. We should tune in to them, try to understand what they're going through, and support and comfort them through the changes they're experiencing.

Parents are the ones who help their children develop their own value system. Previous teachings from parents can play a significant role in shaping their sexual behavior.

In our globalized society, with the constant bombardment of information through music, advertisements, movies, not only is sex promoted in various ways, but also all sorts of pleasures and excesses. People economically benefit from exploiting ignorance and group influence, leading teenagers to indulge in greater consumption of alcohol, drugs, clothing, music, food, and parties.

We, as parents, should explain the risks of such behaviors to our children, as well as the concept of non-consensual sex, the risks of unwanted pregnancies, sexually transmitted diseases, and the effects on their self-esteem when they give in to something they're not fully convinced about. We need to discuss the feelings of guilt that can arise and that they might have to navigate. The most important task during this stage is to teach them to take care of themselves and to respect themselves.

As parents, we should trust them and be confident that they will put into practice what we've taught them. We can't be with them all the time, so we need to convey that we believe they can handle situations well.

Sexual arousal and curiosity can be exploited by older individuals to initiate sexual activities without their consent, and this is considered "sexual abuse".

We should instill in them the awareness that they can always say No and that no one can force them to do something they don't want to do.

Prevention lies in making them aware of the dangers, which exist for both girls and boys, although they might be minor.

Regarding abuse, having the right information during this stage makes it less likely to happen.

In closing this chapter, I hope that all the information provided throughout has been useful to the reader and can be put into practice for the better development of human beings, from childhood to adulthood.

Chapter 6

PLAY, SING AND TELL

Gisela Vespa

"Nothing lights up a child's mind like playing."
Dr. Stuart Brown

Playing is very important and is a part of healthy emotional development. It's the natural path to meaningful learning, awakening creativity, encouraging experimentation, and allowing for personal discoveries. It enhances social, cognitive, and communicative development, exercises attention, memory, and concentration. It creates a relaxed atmosphere without hierarchies or pressures.

Most authors who discuss play consider it an innate activity. For a baby, play is life itself. We could say that it's one of the main occupations in childhood, beneficial for cognitive, social, and emotional development. Through play, boys and girls explore and learn, interact, communicate, develop their personalities, motor skills, and abilities. Playing with others promotes the development of their social skills, conflict resolution, and intellectual capacities. Play thus becomes a preparatory exercise for functions that will be necessary in adulthood, such as patience, tolerance for frustration, respect for rules, conflict resolution, communication, use of strategies, and much more…

The history of play is unimaginably ancient. Playful activity reflected the paradigm of each era and then adapted to the advances of the world. Invasions and migrations carried cultures, languages, and customs, but also games. Wars created competitive games, strategy games, which today have become Risk, Battleship, Tic-Tac-Toe, chess, checkers. The time of archery and hunting brought darts, Snakes and Ladders. Even the Yo-Yo, the Chinese invention favored by the Prince of Wales, and wooden puzzles created in Japan indicated that initially it was the adults who played.

Bowling and "taba," although they seem like games of our own, came to us from ancient Greece. In the time of the Aztecs, in Mexico, a game was played with a ball, a kind of basketball where the player could touch the ball with any part of the body except the hands or feet. It had to pass through a narrow stone hoop placed very high on a vertical wall.

There was also a time of prohibition of parlor games in some countries like poker because they were practiced in brothels. In those times, the church intervened in determining what was good and bad, and games like hopscotch were created that started from "earth" to reach "heaven" if you "didn't fall."

The truth is that promoting screen-free play, with family or friends, encourages healthy competition, the struggle to win, relationships, and dealing with failure from losing.

The play according to age

75% of brain development occurs after birth, and play allows for healthy development by generating more neural connections that contribute to comprehensive growth. From the earliest interactions with the baby, the development of social, temporal, and spatial skills is favored. In the first few months of life, where the baby gazes at caregivers and smiles, someone hides and appears behind a blanket, or a rattle is shaken. Similarly, stimulating with a rattle from one side to the other allows for visual and/or auditory tracking of the object.

Functional Play and Exploratory Play: During the first six months approximately, babies perform spontaneous and uncoordinated movements with their hands, arms, and legs. As they master these movements through repetition, they will begin to discover objects by taking them in their hands and bringing them to their mouths. Exploration is undoubtedly the quintessential mode in this stage, where they use their senses to explore; everything becomes a surprise, and the simplest things become extraordinary. They play with their hands, feet, voice, putting everything in their mouth, exploring with their hands, feet (and their whole body), gradually approaching objects or toys first with their hands, then with hand-eye coordination bringing things to their mouth, crawling, and then crawling or walking to get what they desire. Even when they start complementary feeding around 6 months, they do so by exploring different foods and textures. Getting messy (hands, face, or sometimes the whole body) is part of recognizing their own body and the boundary between the body and the outside world. Undoubtedly, parents are their best playmates, but especially from the fourth or fifth month of a baby's life, they become their primary reference and source of entertainment. In this stage, they start

78

showing interest in communication through babbling, listening attentively when spoken to, and even responding. Sometimes caregivers may find certain behaviors frustrating; however, it's important to know that certain learning processes are taking place behind those behaviors. For example, systematically throwing objects to the ground helps them develop spatial notions and the understanding of a milestone: cause and effect or action-reaction. Play accompanies every stage of development. Freud developed this concept based on "Fort (gone) Da (here)". In this case, around the age of one, play serves as a way for the child's psyche to process, representing real situations experienced: their mother leaves, entrusting them to others, and then returns.

During the first year of life, they engage in simple and repetitive activities that may seem boring to adults but bring them great satisfaction, such as filling a container and then pouring it out or banging blocks together.

How to Support Them: Adults have the role of accompanying these needs by providing safe spaces for exploration. It's important to have a facilitating environment, meaning a space where the baby can be comfortable and secure, encouraging freedom of movement and exploration, free from dangerous or fragile elements. Offer different toys, objects, or materials with various textures that are safe and age-appropriate. Music and movements led by caregivers promote support, attachment, and movement.

Self-Assertion Games: Ages 1 to 2 years: As they start walking and their language skills progressively develop, a new phase begins where they can fend for themselves to get what they want. During this stage, they seek to understand themselves, exploring their possibilities and capabilities. They show interest in discovering their potential and seeking new challenges. They want to do things by themselves, challenge themselves to achieve new milestones, like climbing up or down (from a chair, table, or a step...). They seek the gaze of adults, especially those significant figures, showing what they're doing or inviting others to play with them.

How to Support Them: It's important at this stage to support the development of children's autonomy, as they have a strong desire to imitate what adults do. Whenever possible, allow them to do things themselves, and using affirming words will foster their self-esteem and potential. This age is characterized by egocentrism; they tend to engage in parallel play, not wanting to share or take what others have. Teaching sharing and initiating social skills through shared play is important.

Symbolic and Construction Play: Ages 2 to 4 years. At this age, children most enjoy construction and subsequent destruction games. Their interest in construction arises from their need to organize the world according to their own rules. Destruction arises from their desire to demonstrate their abilities and exert control. They also start engaging in symbolic play, "pretend play," where they imitate everyday situations like talking on the phone, driving, cooking, feeding babies or dolls, etc. Likewise, they often represent fantastical or unreal scenes, which enhances imagination and creativity development.

Symbolic play also includes singing or inventing songs, riddles, or jokes. Drawing and storytelling are part of this stage too.

How to Support Them: Shared play creating scenes together promotes language development, imagination, and creativity. Sharing stories, songs, rhymes, or riddles and dancing are some options.

Rule-Based Play: Ages 4 to 6 years. Interest in rules begins, along with using their own game rules and enforcing them. There's a greater interest in shared play with others, which promotes social exchange. Associative play leads to the emergence of role-playing games. Children gathered agree beforehand on the roles each will play. This gives rise to the first rule-based activities. Rule-based play is a powerful tool for learning and developing specific skills. Through educational games, children don't feel evaluated or pressured; they actively and enjoyably participate, developing skills such as attention, comprehension, memory, and executive functions like organization, anticipation, planning, and strategic thinking.

How to Support Them: It's an important time to use play to promote patience during waiting times, conflict resolution, tolerance for frustration, emotional management, and setting limits: what's allowed and what's not. Games like memory matching, Chutes and Ladders, checkers, word puzzles, bingo, Uno, dice games, and countless card games are helpful.

Competitive Play: From 7 years onward. At this stage, peers become more important, and children prefer playing with peers rather than adults. Group play typically comes in two modes: competitive and cooperative. Both provide children with extensive knowledge and experiences. Competitive games emerge, which later turn into sports.

These types of games also allow the development of physical skills, coordination, and understanding of limits.

How to Support Them: It's important to help them manage emotions and tolerate the frustrations of winning and losing. It's an opportunity to explore sports and discover abilities and interests.

Nicolás Di Giovanni clearly expresses the significance of play and sports for children and adolescents. In his essay, he talks about the right to play as a catalyst for learning beyond classrooms or homes. He advocates for this right for all children and adolescents, and for adults, especially educators, to be aware of it. He explains that physical education, movement, recreation, and sports contain values and principles that can be applied to daily life, work, studies, or interpersonal relationships. Not only do they instill values, but also on a physiological level, they promote the favorable development of the entire organism. Each system functions better: the cardiovascular and respiratory system improves primarily, and the neuromuscular system forms new connections, enhancing kinesthetic intelligence and providing greater ease in quickly solving motor challenges and even academic challenges in the classroom, such as mathematics, language, science, and more.

The play as a catalyst for Classroom Learning

Play elicits pleasure through the release of endorphins, oxytocin, and dopamine in the brain, reinforcing neural connections and improving information storage or long-term memory, which in turn affects working memory. The release of these neurotransmitters also alleviates anxiety and stress, producing feelings of confidence and bonding.

Learning through play also promotes the proper development of inhibitory control, crucial for mental flexibility, impulse control, and emotion regulation. Today, neuroscience tells us that motivation, attention, and memory are activated when we engage in activities that excite us. Achieving this excitement greatly enhances the potential for learning. Games trigger excitement in students, motivating them, and also encourage curiosity, which fosters learning. They are also an excellent way to strengthen intra and interpersonal relationships. Connecting with students through their interests or familiar topics enhances the bond with their teachers and their willingness to acquire new knowledge.

Music is also an essential channel that contributes to well-being, bodily movement, and knowledge retention. Music can be used in various ways: for relaxation, working on rhymes or riddles, recognizing sounds of letters, numbers, animals, languages, cultural elements, and other content. It's used to work on rhythm, coordination, and bodily expression, among other things. It's not solely about the subject "Music," but about utilizing this resource in any subject area with the objectives the teacher sets.

Singing, dancing, or copying simple choreographies develop creativity, musical ear, and visuomotor skills in children. When done in groups, it cultivates bodily connections, time-space coordination, patience, and modesty. Similarly, drawing, painting, and crafts refine fine motor skills and lay the groundwork for reading and writing.

Some Suggestions:

- Play Corner or Peace Corner: Depending on the age of the students, you can create a corner in the classroom with various activities that invite them to work on different functions in a relaxed space. These spaces could include riddles, playdough, word building, puzzles, a calm-down jar, instructions for origami, posters with child-friendly breathing techniques, etc.

- Breathing as an Anchor: Teach students to pay attention and observe how the air enters and exits their nose. You can ask them to count each breath or to say a word or phrase with each inhalation and exhalation.

- Music and Body Expression.

- Icebreaker Games when starting a new topic.

- Story Time: Reading stories to children before bedtime not only stimulates sleep but also provides a secure bond. As children grow, they can retell the story to adults or create new stories, stimulating memory and creativity.

The era of technology

Television started a journey into entertainment five generations ago, especially as it entered homes and gave way to screens in the hands of children, freeing us from street insecurities and changing the way we socialize and define friendship. Playing alone on screens online does not allow for physical sharing and generally fosters more aggressive competition. Today, through various studies, we can understand the enormous negative impact screens have on the holistic development of children and adolescents. In cognitive development, screens have a negative impact on language development, attention, concentration, emotional regulation, impulse control, and social skills. The earlier the age of starting screen use and the more exposure to screens, the greater the impact on children and adolescents development.

In terms of mental health, screens affect the quality and quantity of sleep, promote sedentary behavior and obesity, lead to poor posture, affecting oxygenation and vision development. An increasing number of children need glasses at a young age due to screen use.

Moreover, screen use can affect the dopaminergic circuit, leading to addiction, anxiety, and depression. Other problems associated with technology use and social media include body image disturbance, leading to disorders such as bulimia, anorexia, and body dysmorphic disorder; distortion of sexuality when encountering pornography and sexualized content at an age when they are not prepared or educated about it; cyberbullying and grooming, challenges that can lead to self-harm or suicide, among others.

For many parents, the use of technological devices has become a tool to "entertain" children when waiting, to keep them "quiet" during family gatherings, or even to calm crying or tantrums. This use of technology actually hinders emotional expression and emotion management, which need to be nurtured and taught to children and adolescents. While they may appear "quiet," they are actually placed in a passive state, receiving many stimuli without the opportunity to interact with others, thereby reducing frustration tolerance, patience, creativity, and socialization skills.

In an era where we are surrounded by various technological devices, social media, and applications, it is recommended that screen use be mediated and controlled by an adult, with limited usage time that can be predetermined and agreed upon with children and adolescents.

Chapter 7

CONSCIOUS NUTRITION

Stella García

Thinking about Nutrition as Holistic Health

We define the human being as a bio-psycho-socio-spiritual unity. In other words, it consists of biological, psychological, social, and spiritual dimensions. We can also say that, from an integral perspective, it comprises three components: body, soul, and spirit.

This human being functions as an entirety, an irreducible whole, a biological, mental, emotional, social, and spiritual unity. It has unique ways of functioning and relating to its environment, influenced by culture, historical context, and the place it inhabits.

To cultivate the inherent wholeness in a harmonious manner, it will be necessary to care for and pay attention to each of the areas: body, soul, and spirit. In doing so, we will be taking care of our holistic health.

When we refer to the concept of *Holistic Health*, we define it as the subjective homeostasis or equilibrium experienced in each area of the human being: body, soul, and *spirit*. This means that it will be the task of each human being, if they want to experience and sustain their holistic health over time - which will be a daily task and challenge - to care for each of these constituent areas, providing attention, quality time, and resources to their needs, from each element.

For instance, attending to and meeting the needs of the *body*, such as balanced, nutritious, and conscious nutrition, seven to eight hours of daily rest, physical exercise, routine medical and dental check-ups, personal hygiene and aesthetics as well as maintaining a clean living environment, exposure to sunlight and connection with nature, among others.

When discussing the care of the *soul*, we are referring to designing and building a personal, free, and independent life project. This includes achieving dreams and aspirations, maintaining healthy interpersonal relationships - be it family, romantic, work-related, friendships, colleagues, etc. It involves nurturing creativity and leisure, fulfilling responsibilities, work, and goals. Taking care of the quality of our thoughts, feelings, and behaviors, and reflecting on questions like: What do I want for my life? How would I like to be?

Lastly, paying attention to the needs of the *spirit*, starting by addressing the existential questions: Who is God to me? How can I have a personal and healthy relationship with HIM?

The outcome for a human being, after reflecting on how they are faring in each of the areas that comprise them, analyzing their lifestyle, and reevaluating how much time they invest in one area at the expense of others, should motivate us to envision our life platform. This is the life we desire to lead once we have finished analyzing our current state and have identified the elements that need to be present on that life platform. This is what will help us function *healthily* and in *balance*. In other words, we move closer to a platform of holistic health where there is harmony and equilibrium in the dynamics of the three components - body, soul, and spirit. This harmony and equilibrium, known as "shalom" - the harmony or equilibrium resulting in peace among the three components of the human being - gives rise to the sought-after *inner peace*.

This inner peace can be experienced not from external modifications but through structuring internal changes that arise from evaluating one's current life situation.

The key question that arises is: What could I modify or improve to get closer to a platform of holistic health? How can I take care of all three parts in an integral manner? And then, taking action to bring about these changes!

When an individual experiences Holistic Health, being the bio-psycho-socio-spiritual unity that they are, they also experience a psychological concept that we call *Psychological Well-being*. This refers to the sensation or perception of feeling or experiencing well-being in five areas: physical, mental, emotional, social, and spiritual.

Psychological well-being is the way of life that leads individuals to feel content with themselves. It involves the development of potentials and strengths that allow the individual to establish an effective and satisfactory relationship with themselves and the environment around them, granting them a sense of well-being, tranquility, and joy.

Where Happiness and Psychological Well-being Converge

Happiness is an emotion that is closely tied to the outcome of psychological well-being. It is one of the emotions that reflects this state of well-being. Others include feelings of tranquility, stability, and harmony.

Now, how significant is the role of nutrition in this state of psychological well-being and as a factor related to cultivating holistic health?

Mindful Eating

It's said that through the *body*, one can experience the physical world; through the *soul*, one can know oneself; and through the *spirit*, one can know God.

The body has five organs corresponding to the five senses, allowing humans to communicate with the physical world. It's the means through which we engage with our environment and interact within it. With nature, animals, and everything around us... including food!

When we talk about *mindful eating*, we are referring to the involvement of these five senses in the act of consuming food. It's about becoming aware of how good or nutritious the food we're consuming is, whether it's a free choice made during adolescence and adulthood or guided by adults for children, especially in childhood when adults are responsible for children's nutrition at home.

Mindful Eating involves applying mindfulness to the act of eating, directing *attention* and *intention* to the experience of thoughts, emotions, physical sensations, and behaviors that take place before, during, and after eating.

It's a way of engaging with food that invites rediscovering a *healthy and joyful relationship with what we eat*. Mindful eating means paying attention to what we're doing, becoming aware of *what we eat, how much we eat, how we eat, and why we eat*. Understanding our eating patterns is crucial for maintaining healthy nutrition.

However, eating mindfully doesn't mean restricting food consumption or adhering to a strict diet. Quite the opposite: it aims to transform eating into something enjoyable rather than a temptation or a source of regret. It's about finding pleasure in the simple act of eating.

Therefore, it represents a shift in our relationship with food from within ourselves. It involves our body, mind, emotions, and choices - behaviors - in the preparation and consumption of food.

With this paradigm, focused on becoming aware of what we consume, the goal is for each of us to be fully conscious of what we eat at every moment, savor it, enjoy it, and simultaneously provide our body with exactly what it needs, no more and no less. This is why we also end up talking about *mindful nutrition*; the intake of food is intended to provide the necessary doses of vitamins, minerals, proteins, water, and other nutrients for the optimal functioning of the human body.

What's happening with the media nowadays? It bombards people with a vast array of food options, many of which are minimally nutritious or even detrimental to human health.

Furthermore, it's undeniable that distractions have diverted our attention to televisions, computers, and smartphones while eating.

As a result, eating has become a seemingly senseless act, often performed hastily and concurrently with other parallel activities.

Eating has turned into a mindless action, often rushed and done in conjunction with other simultaneous activities. Throughout our learning journey - both as children, teenagers, and adults - we've internalized dysfunctional patterns in relation to food, giving eating the power to fulfill needs unrelated to hunger. Almost everyone can recall instances where they've eaten out of boredom, loneliness, social pressure, or simply because food is available.

These patterns of eating, unrelated to the internal cues of hunger and satiety, underlie many of the behaviors surrounding eating that are prevalent among children, teenagers, and adults today. The younger generations are often influenced by the adult models they encounter daily.

There are three eating styles: *restrictive*, associated with a diet mentality of prohibition and scarcity, which is unsustainable in the medium and long term, as restricting certain types of foods often triggers the desire to consume them; *emotional*, which involves using food to manage emotions; and *external eating*, which occurs when the desire to eat is triggered by external cues such as the presence of food, smells, colors, etc.

These eating styles themselves aren't inherently problematic; the real issue is the significant lack of *attention* and *disconnection* with ourselves and our bodies. This is why mindful eating proposes a model where our relationship with food is based on paying attention to our internal signals, balancing three fundamental forces: satisfaction, understood as pleasure and well-being; care, encompassing attention to our physical, psychological, emotional, and social needs; and health.

This practice involves:

• Eating slowly.

• Avoiding distractions while eating.

• Recognizing and paying attention to physical hunger cues.

• Stopping eating when feeling satisfied.

• Differentiating between true hunger triggers, appetite triggers, and emotional hunger triggers.

• Engaging your senses by noticing the colors, smells, sounds, textures, and flavors of the food.

• Learning to cope with guilt and anxiety before and after eating.

• Eating to improve overall health and well-being.

• Noticing the effects that food has on your emotions.

• Fully and gratefully appreciating your food.

This practice allows you to replace automatic thoughts and reactions with more conscious and healthy responses, enhancing your overall well-being and health.

Nutrition, Brain, and Mood

I'm sure you've found yourself in a situation more than once where you turned to certain, generally unhealthy foods to soothe an emotion and seek a state of pleasure. Let me give you an example. One day, you come home from work stressed and tired, you open the pantry, and oh, there's chocolate! You eat them quickly, barely chewing or savoring, achieving a sense of satisfaction and calm. However, after a while, feelings of guilt and emotional discomfort creep in. As a result, it leads us to either restrictive behavior or impels us to seek another dose of sugar or refined flour to regain that sensation. This example prompts us to reflect on how the relationship between our mood and eating occurs.

The human brain has very high energy demands, with highly specialized nutritional requirements. Naturally, this means that good nutritional status is crucial for mental health. If the nutritional quality of the foods we consume is deficient, it can contribute to impaired brain function or mood.

From the scientific community's perspective, there's a notable prevalence of high consumption of sugars, refined flours, and gluten in today's diet. These three elements promote chronic inflammation and are linked to being a factor that contributes to mental disorders and various other organic disease.

Studies have been conducted on individuals with various types of mental disorders, and on average, deficiencies in the following nutrients have been found:

- Polyunsaturated fatty acids (found in fish and plant oils).

- Minerals like zinc (found in meats, grains, legumes, and dairy), magnesium (found in leafy green vegetables, nuts, and grains), iron (found in red meat, leafy green vegetables, eggs, some fruits).

- Vitamins, such as B vitamins (found in leafy green vegetables, fortified cereals, dairy, yeast, and grains), and antioxidant vitamins like C and E (found in fruits and vegetables).

McLean Hospital, affiliated with Harvard University, conducted a study on the relationship between depression and food, published on April 15, 2005, in the "Issue of Biological Psychiatry." Researchers found that Omega-3 fatty acids and foods high in uridine - such as sugar cane extract, broccoli, tomatoes, liver, breast milk, and barley - are capable of reducing depression symptoms to an equal or even greater extent than three different antidepressant medications used in the study. These nutrients are also present in fish, nuts, and molasses, among other foods.

In another study titled "Changing Diets, Changing Minds," researchers argue that a wide range of nutrients is essential for the brain and mental health. These nutrients work together to allow the brain to develop and function properly. According to this study, a diet rich in fruits, vegetables, whole grains, cereals, legumes, nuts, seeds, lean meats, and fish oil helps maintain a healthy body and protects against certain diseases. Conversely, a diet containing too many unhealthy elements or lacking essential nutrients is likely to affect brain function and consequently mental health.

McLean Hospital, affiliated with Harvard University, conducted a There are foods rich in two amino acids - small building blocks of proteins - called tryptophan and tyrosine. These are precursors to *serotonin* and *dopamine*, respectively.

Consuming foods rich in these two amino acids can help maintain a consistently elevated level of these hormones. Additionally, other nutrients that influence mental health include calcium, vitamin B complex, potassium, magnesium, and omega-3 fatty acids, among others. Lastly, a fundamental element to consider is adequate water consumption.

On the contrary, foods high in excessive sugar and fats, although often preferred in certain moments, are the least beneficial for our mental health.

There's a specific scientific field that examines the relationship between nutrition and social, emotional, and mental health, known as Nutritional Psychiatry. In this field, experts emphasize how diet and nutrition impact how people feel mentally and emotionally. They also highlight the importance of supporting mental health treatments with dietary and lifestyle changes - such as exercise and connecting with nature.

Indeed, the foods we consume have effects not only on the brain but also on the rest of our *body*. This means that our dietary choices affect not only the brain but also the gastrointestinal system - the intestine - as they are interconnected.

Within the human body, there are around 40 trillion bacteria, most of which reside in the intestine and are known as the gut microbiota. These microorganisms play crucial roles in the body, such as synthesizing neurotransmitters that send chemical messages to the brain to regulate sleep, pain, appetite, mood, and emotions. This is why the intestine is often referred to as the "second brain.".

Technically, the formal name for this relationship, according to experts, is the gut-brain connection or gut-brain axis. Research suggests that the foods we eat influence the health of gut microbiota colonies, which in turn interact with our brain and thus impact our mental and emotional health.

In this context, specialists have identified that certain dietary patterns can help reduce symptoms of depression, anxiety, and overall mood. A significant number of scientific studies have identified links between dietary patterns, gut health, and the risk of depression. One study even found that a diet rich in fruits, vegetables, whole grains, and legumes, and low in red and processed meats, was associated with a 10% lower likelihood of experiencing depressive symptoms.

This type of diet emphasizes increased consumption of fruits, vegetables, fish, nuts, legumes, and olive oil. In contrast, it limits fried foods, processed meats, baked goods, sugary beverages, alcohol, caffeine, and added sugars, all of which can exacerbate anxiety symptoms.

In conclusion, it can be affirmed that a balanced diet can become an ideal ally to improve mood. It involves high-quality, conscious eating rich in a variety of nutrients that promote overall health. Here are some tips:

1. *Incorporate Nutrients:*

- Omega-3 fatty acids (walnuts, chia and flaxseeds, salmon, herring, sardines)

- Folic acid (beef liver, rice, fortified cereals, black-eyed peas, spinach, asparagus, Brussels sprouts)

- Iron (oysters, beef liver, fortified cereals, spinach, dark chocolate, white beans, lentils, tofu)

- Magnesium (spinach, pumpkin and chia seeds, soy milk, black beans, almonds, cashews, peanuts)

- Zinc (oysters, chicken, pork chops, beef roast, Alaskan king crab, lobster, pumpkin seeds)

- B vitamins (chicken breast, beef liver, clams, tuna, salmon, chickpeas, potatoes, bananas)

- Vitamin A (beef liver, herring, cow's milk, ricotta cheese, sweet potatoes, carrots, cantaloupe)

- Vitamin C (red and green peppers, orange and grapefruit juice, strawberries, broccoli).

2. *Prebiotics and Probiotics*: Prebiotics are foods that provide nourishment to the bacteria already living in the intestine, while probiotics contain healthy bacteria. Consuming a diet that includes both helps maintain a balanced state of gut homeostasis. According to some research, these can play a role in the body's response to stress and depression. Foods containing them include:

- Fermented foods like yogurt, kefir, buttermilk, kimchi,

sauerkraut, kombucha

- Garlic, onions, and leeks

- Vegetables like artichokes and asparagus

- Fruits like apples and bananas

- Grains like barley and oats

By paying attention to your diet and incorporating these nutrients, prebiotics, and probiotics, you can support your overall well-being and mental health. Remember, a mindful and balanced approach to nutrition can have a positive impact on your mood and overall quality of life.

3. *Fruits and Vegetables*: These foods are rich in many nutrients that support mental health, including fiber, complex carbohydrates, vitamin B, vitamin C, and healthy plant chemicals called polyphenols. A recent review analyzed 61 studies evaluating fruit intake and mental health, highlighting that consuming more fruits and vegetables is associated with higher levels of optimism and self-efficacy, and lower levels of depression and psychological distress. Some fruits and vegetables that can positively affect mental health include berries, red fruits, blueberries, citrus fruits, and leafy green vegetables.

4. *Whole Grains*: Examples of whole grains include brown rice, buckwheat, and oats, among others. These grains are left entirely intact during processing, retaining more fiber and nutrients compared to refined grains, from which some parts of the plant have been removed. Increased dietary fiber intake is linked to a lower risk of anxiety, depression, and psychological distress. Furthermore, the type of fiber found in whole grains can have anti-inflammatory effects when digested in the intestine, thereby benefiting mental health through the gut-brain axis.

By incorporating a variety of fruits, vegetables, and whole grains into your diet, you can support your mental well-being and contribute to a more balanced and positive state of mind. Remember that nutrition plays a crucial role in maintaining both physical and mental health, and making mindful food choices can have a significant impact on your overall quality of life.

Role of Parents in Children and Adolescents' Nutrition

Parents and teachers serve as role models, where their actions, language, and attitude set the guidelines for the development of infants and adolescents, such as in routines that contribute to forming eating habits.

It's worth mentioning that during development, children and adolescents exhibit different patterns of food acceptance that are deeply influenced by various factors such as the family's socio-economic status, the child's health, climate, environment, food availability and accessibility, and the parents' age and culture, coupled with the caregiver's food preferences and family eating habits.

Therefore, the family is considered the primary influencer in children's eating practices, which can shape their future food preferences. As a result, both dietary patterns and relationships with food are established. Eating habits acquired during childhood have consequences on physical development and dietary choices in later stages.

The question of the role parents play in developing eating habits in their children has gained increasing importance, becoming a topic of worldwide interest. The World Health Organization and the International Obesity Task Force, part of the International Association for the Study of Obesity, have prioritized research into the influence of parenting styles on children's eating behaviors and healthy behaviors.

Given the significance of parents' and caregivers' role in establishing these habits from early childhood, the parental objective becomes not only to ensure their child's health today but also to help them acquire a set of habits that promote autonomy in their eating choices as they become young adults. This way, they can continue making good choices, maintaining good health, and fostering a healthy relationship with food and their bodies.

This is why the question arises, "How can I help my child develop these healthy habits?" Here are some tips:

1. Teach them to respect their body's signals.

A key factor, which might surprise us as adults since we often forget it ourselves, is allowing our child to listen to the hunger and fullness signals their body sends. It's challenging for us to trust these signals because as adults, we often believe we know how much our child should eat at any given moment. When we see them deviate from our expectations, conflict arises, and we start trying to control their eating.

2. Offer them healthy foods.

The foods we provide should be healthy and suitable for them. In other words, we need to limit the availability of unhealthy products in our home. We are responsible for ensuring that the food in front of our child is appropriate and nutritious.

This may seem obvious, but in practice, it's not easy. A quick trip to any supermarket will show a variety of enticing, convenient, and visually appealing foods that are not healthy. Making good choices can be a challenge, especially because children's products often feature bright colors, characters, or games that make them very appealing. It might be difficult as parents to say no in these situations. However, if we remain consistent in buying only what we believe is suitable and saying no to requests for unhealthy products, this will gradually become a habit. Over time, our child will learn to accept it with less frustration..

3.   Be a model of healthy eating.

One of the primary ways children and adolescents learn is through observation of role models, especially their parents, who are their fundamental reference points. For this reason, instilling good eating habits in our children can be challenging if they observe us eating unhealthily.

The first step is to improve your own eating habits. Let's take the initiative to consume healthy foods as something natural and habitual, exhibit self-control when consuming less healthy products, and ensure that our home only contains nutritious foods.

4.   Provide appropriate time for eating.

We are aware that children do things more slowly than adults. They are also easily distracted, prone to making mistakes, or getting messy. However, sometimes our patience (or planning) fails us, and we expect them to behave like adults. We might schedule tight timelines for meals, wake them up at the last minute, and then become stressed when we realize we're running late for school, they're getting messy, or they're getting distracted. What's worse is that the solution we often find is to take charge ourselves or "make things easier" for them: we feed them (to save time), provide them with less messy products (whether they are the best for them or not), thus limiting their development in this area.

What can we do then? When organizing daily routines, take into account and anticipate the time the child or adolescent will need to eat or complete any task. All of this will contribute to making mealtime a calmer and more relaxed environment, instead of a stressful moment where everyone is in a rush, feeling frustrated and angry because things are not going as desired or imagined.

5.   Make mealtime enjoyable.

In today's fast-paced and postmodern society, finding time for everyone to sit down and eat together is becoming increasingly challenging. However, this remains a very healthy habit for the entire family and especially for children.

Transforming mealtimes into moments of connection among family members can help children observe how their parents eat and learn from them as role models. It also provides an opportunity to have everyday and frequent conversations with them, which is increasingly necessary for the emotional development of our children. The central idea is to make the most of the time while ensuring it's a pleasant moment without arguments or conflicts, but rather a relaxed time to share and enjoy being together.

In this way, children can associate food and the act of eating with something positive, pleasurable, and enjoyable.

It becomes a moment of mindful eating, where, as mindfulness teaches us, the challenge is to be present—mind, body, and spirit—fully connected to the human experience of eating..

*Here's to many more of these moments of mindful
nourishment in our everyday lives!*

What happens when developing a healthy relationship with food becomes difficult?

In many instances, when our parents fail to teach or guide us, our approach to eating and our relationship with food can lead to various issues. It's important to note that difficulties that arise in the parent-child relationship, especially with the maternal figure—who symbolizes the provider of nourishment from the womb through the umbilical cord and continues to be the primary figure in feeding and nurturing the infant and child—can profoundly affect how those children develop their connection with food. This extends to the parents themselves, who bring their own ways of relating to food rooted in emotional connections with their own maternal and paternal figures, which then become models for their children.

A valuable question to ask ourselves in order to understand our current relationship with food could be: What kind of emotional connection do I have with my maternal figure? How was the bond formed between her and me? How was I treated by her? How did I feel when she was around? What memories do I have of her role when I was a child? Do these memories evoke pleasant emotions or, conversely, are they traumatic memories that bring forth uncomfortable emotions in me?

We are discussing behavioral inheritances here—deep-seated habits from childhood, patterns of behavior, cultural ways of organizing family eating, preferences for certain food groups over others, culinary traditions, and approaches to meal planning for breakfast, lunch, dinner, and snacks.

This is a significant topic for analysis, as it could be the origin of numerous imbalances and disorders related to eating, such as:

Anorexia Nervosa: It is an eating disorder characterized by a restriction of food intake, resulting in significant weight loss. Often, children or adolescents with anorexia maintain a weight below the expected minimum for their age, sex, or developmental stage, and in some cases, it leads to severe malnutrition. In many instances, these individuals engage in risky behaviors to lose weight, such as excessive exercise to rapidly burn calories, using laxatives or diuretics, or inducing vomiting. It's crucial for adults to pay attention to these behaviors and seek help from professionals in psychology and nutrition who specialize in this area.

Bulimia: In this disorder, children or adolescents experience episodes where they cannot regulate the compulsion to consume large amounts of food in a short period. To compensate for this binge-eating, they often resort to vomiting or using laxatives. The onset of bulimia typically occurs between late adolescence and early adulthood (between 18 and 25 years old), and it is more common among women.

There are two subtypes of bulimia, based on the behaviors following a binge-eating episode:

Purging-Type Bulimia: This subtype involves episodes of binge-eating followed by self-induced vomiting. Often, the individual uses their fingers to induce vomiting. They tend to do this in secret to avoid detection by others during binge-eating or vomiting episodes. The use of laxatives or diuretics also falls under purging-type bulimia.

Non-Purging Bulimia: In this case, binge-eating episodes are not followed by vomiting or laxative use. Instead, compensatory behaviors may include excessive physical exercise or fasting.

It might be confusing for parents to differentiate between anorexia and bulimia. Here are some general differences that can help in family prevention:

- In anorexia nervosa, there is low body weight (underweight), while in bulimia, individuals typically have normal weight or even overweight.

- In anorexia nervosa, there is excessive control over the food consumed, whereas in bulimia, loss of control occurs during binge-eating episodes.

- Although purging-type anorexia exists, the key distinction is that purging behaviors in anorexia occur without excessive food intake, whereas in bulimia, they always follow a binge-eating episode.

- Regarding the age of onset, anorexia tends to manifest in early adolescence, while bulimia often appears in late adolescence or early adulthood.

Avoidant/Restrictive Food Intake Disorder: This is an eating disorder where a child or adolescent has little interest in food or actively avoids it. As a result, they often lose a significant amount of weight or fail to gain weight as expected for their age.

What's notable about this disorder is that individuals who experience it don't have a fear of gaining weight, nor do they possess a negative or distorted body image of themselves. They simply don't eat because they find the *smell, taste, texture, or color of food unpleasant.* They might have a fear of vomiting and/or choking on food and suffering from aspiration, but they don't have anorexia nervosa, bulimia nervosa, or another medical issue that could explain their eating-related behavior.

Childhood and Adolescent Obesity: The causes of obesity are not solely related to individual or family factors such as genetics, eating habits, and physical activity within a family's culture. They also encompass multiple and complex situations in the broader environment that can contribute to obesity. Some examples include:

- Unfair food systems and economic factors that can make it difficult for some families to access or afford more nutritious and healthy food options for their child's growth.

- Unsafe physical environments that can limit opportunities for physical activity, exercise, or active play outdoors.

- Chronic sources of stress that a family may experience. This type of stress can affect the endocrine system, which regulates hormones that, in turn, play a role in regulating weight and have other effects on health.

With all the above in mind, it's a call to action to work towards creating a better environment where all children and families can grow up healthy and balanced on a comprehensive level. However, until we can establish healthier environments, let's remember that treatment for overweight and obesity, anorexia, and bulimia can still be effective despite unhealthy surroundings.

It's essential for parents to seek help from professional teams that can support both them and their children. Child and adolescent psychologists specializing in eating disorders, pediatricians, nutritionists, fitness trainers, or other sports and recreational institutions should be the primary sources of support.

Cognitive-behavioral therapy (CBT) has been proven highly effective for these disorders, as it yields better results in alleviating symptoms and overall recovery. Group therapy is also important, both for the child or adolescent and their closest family members. It allows them to identify with others and move away from isolation, while collectively relearning new, more functional and healthy eating patterns to implement as a family.

Let's not forget that starting the prevention of eating disorders from childhood is important, fostering the development of self-esteem and healthy eating patterns. Learning to eat mindfully and healthily is a task for all of us, and it's a beautiful challenge to care for our holistic health.

Chapter 8

MOTOR AND SENSORIAL DISABILITIES

Victoria A. Burgenik

When addressing the topic of disability, something very specific happens in every aspect of everyday life: home, school, work, neighborhood. Sadly, it's a taboo subject, but it's becoming increasingly addressed in society. Little by little, people with disabilities are being recognized as subjects with rights, but the journey ahead is long and challenging.

No one is prepared in life to receive a diagnosis of disability for oneself, a family member, or a loved one. A growing belly during pregnancy is always accompanied by the dream that "it doesn't matter if it's a boy or a girl, as long as they are born healthy" (and if they come with a loaf of bread under their arm, even better). The problem arises when, in the delivery room, the doctor is left speechless because the child was clearly born with a disability or something caused it after birth..

Even more so when someone who has completely conventional health suddenly experiences an accident, a seizure, or another unexpected incident that turns their life upside down. The Bible recommends that we approach those with disabilities with love, respect, and faith that God knows all things, His plan is perfect, even though we don't fully understand it. In the Gospel of Mark (2:1-12), some of God's purposes with a paralyzed man are described, making it clear that those who have a disability are not a result of their own or others' sin (see Gospel of John 9:3). That disability is part of His Divine Plan. It provides evidence that they are His perfect creation (Exodus 4:10-11 mentions someone with speech difficulties, a blind person, a mute person). They are all His creation.

As a community, we often fail not out of malice but out of ignorance. Is it easier to promise divine healing to the deaf person rather than engaging, learning sign language, and bringing the Word to that person who doesn't hear in their own language, just as Jesus did?

The Family and Disability

The family's initial reaction to a child's disability, whether during pregnancy, at birth, or at any point in life, is usually one of shock. Receiving this news from doctors is often met with denial, rejection, and even doubt. A multitude of medical tests and consultations typically follow which usually confirm the diagnosis.

Then comes a stage of profound pain, depression, guilt, and anger – all of which are normal in any grieving process. Life becomes disorganized, each family member navigates the process as best they can and within the timeframe allowed by their own psychological structure. When there are siblings of the individual with a disability, they also need psychological and spiritual attention. Parents must seek answers to questions they never anticipated, which intensifies their distress. However, this process can also strengthen their resolve to hope that living with this reality will make them more human, understanding, tolerant, and loving. Delaying the start of this process, just to avoid pain, will only generate more anguish.

Transforming "Why me?" or "Why my child?" or "Why my family?" into "Why not me?" or "What is the purpose of this?" might be the beginning of healing for the soul. Finding that we can turn our pain into hope for ourselves and other families is the most comforting realization. Embracing another parent in the emergency room who has just experienced a life-altering moment, forever shifting their path, makes every tear worthwhile.

When a family member with a disability appears, we learn to value the simplest and everyday things that we previously did not appreciate or celebrate: the moment our child took a step supported by their crutches, our daughter gripping a crayon to draw, or being able to communicate their feelings. We become capable of understanding a language that was once distant, confusing, or unknown.

When adolescence comes

If adolescence is challenging for any parent, imagine what it's like when your child has a disability. They battled with the disability and faced questions they never thought they'd need to address in parenthood, and that struggle will continue stronger in this stage.

Adolescence is about anguish. It's the mourning of childhood fading away and the anxiety of not having answers to what they're experiencing and feeling. This is even more true for a young person with a visual, auditory, or motor limitation. Hormones surge: beards grow, voices deepen, acne appears, and in girls, breasts develop and menstruation starts. Maintaining an open channel of communication with teenagers is essential. If they could share their childhood mischiefs, they can share what they're going through now.

It's important for them to understand that they can be heard without judgment, that the lines of communication are open, and they won't be judged for their feelings or fears. In peer groups, if integration was successful in childhood, teasing and mockery are unlikely during this phase. However, if there's a change in social circles due to a new school, church, club, or neighborhood, it's crucial to sensitize peers so that they don't mistreat the teenager with a disability.

Often, jokes can be cruel and damage the self-esteem of a young person with physical limitations. It's never too late to sensitize the group to which they belong if it hasn't been done before. Lead them to empathize with someone who is blind or deaf. Blindfolding someone for a while will help them understand the blind person's perspective and prevent humiliation. Putting themselves in someone else's shoes will make a difference.

In summary, work on raising awareness in the social groups of the person with a disability; listen to the adolescent with any disability and try to understand their fears, anxieties, and dreams; encourage and support them during this stage; educate yourself, participate in workshops, seminars, or conferences on the topic; organize activities for adolescents with disabilities where everyone can integrate, and collaborate with other parents who are going through the same stage to form support groups to address fears, clarify doubts, and celebrate achievements.

Guidelines for Teachers

It's crucial to understand that Children and Adolescents with Disabilities are a perfect creation of God and not a mistake of nature. It's important to know that they are part of the divine plan and that they too have been called to believe in and share the good news.

NGOs, clubs, churches, and organizations that work with children and adolescents should seek training so that they are prepared when a child with a disability arrives, or even to detect if they notice any difficulties in a child within their group. Sometimes parents deny reality and overlook situations that should be consulted with a pediatrician as soon as possible: children who can't walk, talk, sit, manipulate objects, or tie their shoelaces at an expected age. A child might seem shy, but they could also not socialize due to being deaf. Everyone is talking and gesturing, but they don't understand what's happening around them. Perhaps a child walks hesitantly, knocking things over due to unclear vision and is labeled as clumsy. These cases should be consulted with a professional, as they could be the first signs of a condition.

A space dedicated to children and adolescents with disabilities

In community institutions such as clubs, charities, or churches, you may have a group of people with disabilities and their families who participate in your activities. They could be many or few – that doesn't matter. What's important is the quality of the service you provide, so consider the following points:

- Maintain consistency and faithfulness in your task. Families will expect the scheduled gathering; if you interrupt or are inconsistent, people won't know whether to attend or not, and they might give up on participating, feeling once again let down.

- Keep a clear and predictable routine. Don't change the agenda based on your convenience. If you meet when you have a free time slot in your week, families won't know how to organize the next gathering or whether it will even take place. Plan and prioritize this activity in your schedule. Being predictable about the meeting day encourages new people in your organization to attend regularly.

- Don't overload the agenda. Maintain a time commitment that you and your collaborators can handle. Meeting daily might seem commendable, but no one can sustain this in the long run unless it's a paid task.

- Don't abandon the task. It would be frustrating for you, your collaborators, and the families you assist if the task is abandoned. Having several collaborators is essential to cover the agreed-upon time slots.

- Allow yourself time for rest and gather strength for the next activity. Seek wisdom from God, plan, do what's within your reach, and rest in the knowledge that Christ can accomplish what seems impossible. Spend time with your loved ones and include this in your planning.

- Don't be discouraged. Just as Jesus was tossed in a boat during a storm on the sea, his friends let him down, and he had to feed a multitude with five loaves and two fish. Rest in the belief that God can provide everything necessary.

Tips for Interacting

Sometimes we think we can handle a situation because we once helped a person with low vision or blindness on the street. Thinking about some important aspects beforehand when interacting with someone with a disability will help us engage appropriately.

How to assist a child or adolescent with low vision or blindness

- Be descriptive and clear in your language. Words like "this," "that," "here," or "there" are not clear for someone who can't see. Phrases like "in front of you," "to your right," or "the pencil I have in my hand" tend to be clearer.

- Describe the environment where activities are taking place. Let the child become familiar with the surroundings.

- Be predictable; the child will look for their things where they left them. Don't move their belongings without informing them if you need to.

- Speak with the child as if they could see. Don't avoid phrases or words like "see" or "saw." They use them frequently. Be natural.

- Offer your arm or hand to guide the child. Don't take them by the hand; they will feel more secure holding onto you.

- Use tactile materials and adapt activities for them to participate

(e.g., if all children are coloring, they could do a similar activity using textured stickers or other tactile elements)

How to assist a child or adolescent with hearing impairment or deafness

- If the child reads lips, speak to them directly and clearly.

- Learn sign language, as it is the natural language for deaf individuals. If you don't know sign language yet, seek help from an interpreter to communicate.

- Write, use images, drawings, and anything that helps clarify ideas. Electronic device apps can be very helpful for this.

How to assist a child or adolescent with motor difficulties

- Work on removing barriers such as steps or uneven surfaces. If necessary, develop ramps with guidance from architects or qualified personnel. A poorly constructed ramp, even with good intentions, won't be helpful and might waste resources.

- Offer transportation; many times, they face significant challenges in getting to activities due to transportation issues.

- Provide support for daily tasks and errands.

- Plan for an adapted restroom for individuals with motor limitations, following legally applicable building codes. Remember that a centimeter more or less can determine whether the restroom is usable or not.

Lastly, don't forget the following verse: *"The King will reply, 'Truly I tell you, whatever you did for one of the least of these brothers and sisters of mine, you did for me.'" - Matthew 25:40.*

Chapter 9

CHILDREN AND ADOLESCENTS AND THEIR RELATIONSHIP WITH EDUCATION

Stella García

"All problems are education problems."
– Sarmiento –

The passage highlights the paradox of the current situation where, despite significant progress in reducing illiteracy and increasing access to education, there is now a prevalence of what can be termed "emotional illiteracy." This is reflected in the widespread symptomatic behaviors observed in children, adolescents, and adults, which have reached epidemic proportions.

It is not uncommon to hear about or witness instances where students engage in drug and alcohol use, delinquent behavior, disregard for rules, aggression, lack of responsibility towards schoolwork, running away from home, disrespect towards elders, and more.

Within schools, there are students who are easily identifiable or labeled due to their challenging behavior. They become known not only within the classroom but also throughout the entire school community for being defiant, dishonest, restless, disrespectful, and disruptive. This can be frustrating for many and tests the patience of those around them. For those who don't respond positively or submissively to disciplinary measures, they might rebel against these measures and unknowingly choose a path that may not lead to a positive outcome, further entrenching their negative actions and reactions within a system that marginalizes them. This often leads to behaviors extending beyond the school environment.

Furthermore, the passage discusses the challenges that some parents face in raising their children, such as abuse, family fragmentation, parental exhaustion, lack of community support networks in certain areas, urbanization, social insecurity, economic changes, inequality, social marginalization, discrimination, exposure to graphic violence, overcrowded living conditions, and more. All of these factors have an impact on individuals and families.

At the same time, there are cultural and value-related changes that promote consumerism, individualism, materialism, hedonism, relativism, permissiveness, massification, frivolity, the pursuit of immediate pleasure, which adversely influence and make it more challenging to adapt to the current world, both for children and adults.

This is the challenging context of modern education.

This leads to raising the following questions: What can be done for comprehensive education? How can we confront and generate a positive change in children and adolescents, who will be the adults of tomorrow?

These are some questions that spark interest in analyzing the importance of education for teachers, parents, and students, focused on comprehensive education.

Numerous studies demonstrate that children and adolescents who receive comprehensive education, which includes the development of emotional skills, are happier, more confident, and more successful in school and society.

Equally important is the fact that these abilities become the foundation for them to become responsible, attentive, self-assured, and productive adults. The profound importance of these research findings lies in the realization that these emotional skills are entirely learned and capable of being taught. This is where the family - primarily parents - the school, and other institutions tasked with teaching or conveying values - such as churches or religious institutions, among others - should come into play.

It is crucial, then, to consider education as a primary instrument, a generator of harmonious and healthy personal development, which will consequently benefit the community as a whole.

A brief look at the current educational context

"I'm searching for a patch of ground with grass to
place my feet and have my dream.
But everything is burning all around the world, and
we must keep moving".
Gabriela Mistral

Our society is in constant evolution, and as a consequence, the values, expectations, goals, as well as the needs of children and adolescents, are continuously changing.

In the past few decades, education has been undergoing an intriguing paradigm shift. While in the 1990s, it was primarily focused on cognitive development and the acquisition of knowledge, nowadays it has recognized the immense need to perceive humans as integrated beings; that is, considering cognitive, emotional, and moral aspects that interact permanently with the environment.

Humanity is immersed in a rapid process of change that manifests in all spheres of political, social, scientific, and cultural happenings. The context in which businesses operate has undoubtedly changed due to globalization, presenting scenarios different from familiar surroundings. It's in this sense that education is being called upon to adapt and respond to the demands of the times, where emerging opportunities come with new challenges.

Despite the historical tendency for society to overemphasize intelligence at the expense of other individual qualities, empirical evidence has shown that being cognitively intelligent is not sufficient to ensure academic, professional, and personal success.

However, this belief led to schools prioritizing intellectual and academic aspects of students until the late 20th century, convinced that emotional and social aspects were private matters and entirely separate.

In recent decades, there has arisen a need to view education not only as a tool for learning content and developing cognitive competencies but also as a space that contributes to the holistic formation of students. It promotes the construction and reinforcement of values, teaches the cultivation of emotionally healthier lives, and encourages peaceful and harmonious coexistence.

In everyday pedagogical practice, education plays an increasingly necessary and integral role, starting from each child and adolescent's home. Primarily, this responsibility falls on the shoulders of their parents, and secondarily, through the guidance of their teachers.

As Malaisi (2016) adds, there are numerous variables that intersect education today, such as family fragmentation, overcrowded living conditions, rising divorce rates, single-parent and blended families, unintended teenage pregnancies, families with same-sex parents, increased adolescent suicide rates, higher consumption of drugs and alcohol, early initiation of sexual activities, growing rates of repetition and school dropout, economic instability, inequality, marginalization, excessive exposure to graphic violence and dehumanizing technologies, hedonism, image obsession, consumerism, materialism, among other interconnected and interdependent factors that in some way or another affect the current educational landscape.

Due to all these factors, the ultimate goal of professionals in the field of education should be to maximize the students' capacities and skills while also addressing their areas of deficit. Additionally, they should contribute to the holistic development of the students' personalities, ultimately contributing to human development as a whole.

Teaching emotional skills would enhance the psychological and emotional well-being of students, thereby positively impacting both their overall well-being and academic performance.

How children and adolescents learn

This perspective of the life cycle acknowledges that throughout development, there is an allocation of efforts and resources towards different goals at each age. In the case of childhood and adolescence, resources are primarily directed towards the growth and holistic development of the individual during these life stages.

Some General Characteristics of the Childhood Stage (Starting from 6 years old onwards, considering entry into 1st grade in Argentina):

- They reason in a more logical manner.

- They possess a more selective attention and a more secure and strategic memory.

- They greatly expand the quality and quantity of knowledge about various aspects of reality.

- There is a greater development of everyday skills.

- They are capable of orienting themselves in complex spatial paths.

- They are able to understand and remember exact scores, for example, of their favorite soccer teams.

- They can provide accurate testimonies of past events.

- They are capable of understanding humor and irony. That's why, in many cultures, formal education begins in this stage, characterized by a new way of thinking that is more logical and strategic, and by an expansion and better organization of knowledge, which are essential aspects in school learning. The capacity for processing information increases with age. As a result, the limitations of processing decrease with age, leading to more complex cognitive processes. As they grow older, their ability to pay attention and simultaneously relate more units of information also increases, allowing children to engage in more complex cognitive activities. This leads to the development of cognitive skills that are important for academic and personal growth. This results in:

- Increase in processing speed and capacity.

- Development of attention and memory.

- Development of knowledge and metacognition.

These acquisitions are due to the structural changes in the brain (neurological maturation), where the frontal cortex matures and there is greater myelination of nerve pathways. There is also a development of self-esteem, greater understanding, and the development of interpersonal relationships (emergence of reciprocity, representation of other people's mental models, and understanding of others' emotions). Additionally, moral reasoning and the learning of values develop during this stage.

Some general characteristics of the adolescent stage

Adolescence begins with puberty, which refers to a set of physical changes that, over the first and second decades of life, transform the child's body into an adult body capable of reproduction. It is a universal phenomenon. It is a biological fact, unlike adolescence, which is not universal but a cultural construct – meaning that not all cultures experience it.

Adolescence is a cultural product, stemming from the industrial revolution in the late 19th century, when compulsory schooling emerged.

By the end of the 19th century, children entered the workforce sometime between the ages of 7 and the onset of puberty. Few were studying. There was no teenage culture, and adolescence was not perceived as a distinct stage of development. The industrial revolution brought about significant changes; with industrialization, the importance of training, education, and study grew. Although the children of laborers continued to join the workforce at very young ages, the children of the middle and upper classes tended to remain in schools. Schools increased in number, developed specific and more complex programs, and became more demanding. Eventually, the children of laborers also began adopting this lifestyle.

As the century progressed, the concept of *compulsory education* was gradually introduced in Western countries.

Adolescence is a transitional stage, as it's neither childhood nor adulthood. It's a psychosocial period that extends over several years and is characterized by the transition between childhood and adulthood. It begins with puberty and ends when three achievements are reached: economic independence and autonomy, emotional independence, and leaving the parental home.

Psychologist Stanley Hall defined adolescence as "sturm und drang" (storm and stress), considering it a turbulent and troubled period. For Hall, adolescence represented a critical moment in human development. He compared it to the evolutionary stage of humankind, signifying the transition from savagery to civilized society. He believed this period was marked by psychological tensions and distress due to conflicts between adolescent impulses and societal demands.

For the father of psychoanalysis, Sigmund Freud, adolescence marked the end of the latency stage and the resurgence of sexual impulses after puberty. This marked the culmination of psychosexual development: the phase of genital sexuality. The adolescent experiences a resurgence of the Oedipus complex, which they must overcome by emotionally distancing themselves from their parents and turning towards peers. Among these peers, they would choose a socially accepted sexual object (outside the family).

E. Erikson postulated that adolescence was a "Social Moratorium," a period of waiting that society provides to its young members while they prepare to take on adult roles. He regarded adolescence as a crucial period in the development of the self, as the physical, psychological, and social changes would lead the adolescent to an identity crisis. Resolving this crisis would contribute to the consolidation of adult personality.

Psychologist John Coleman, based on interviews with boys and girls aged between 11 and 17 years old, arrives at a conclusion that he outlines in his focal theory.

In this theory, Coleman posits that adolescents must confront new tasks that they must progressively resolve. These tasks involve new roles, commitments, and conflicts that typically don't arise simultaneously but rather sequentially. They are faced at different moments. Thus, the tensions arising from the adolescents' need to respond to new demands and assume new roles are rarely going to occur at the same time.

The significant reflective question that arises, after considering these conceptualizations about adolescence and puberty, is how parents, as well as teachers and educators, are going to accompany these processes of change.

The key lies in accompanying and assisting adolescents during this stage from a place of setting healthy boundaries and parental discipline. This helps frame and reorganize the multitude of changes, preparing them to live in society from a mature adult role. Additionally, it involves firmly educating them in values, cognitive aspects, emotional well-being, spirituality, and physical aspects as well.

Challenges of 21st Century Education

Teaching today should not have the same goals as it did 80 years ago. That's why new practices must be implemented to navigate towards the future with creativity.

In the present day, relying solely on traditional schooling and learning models from 80 years ago is insufficient. The current society, which is ushering in the future "Society 3.0" or the "Knowmad Society" characterized by rapid technological advancements, provides a glimpse of the upcoming demands: individuals who are creative, entrepreneurial, critical thinkers, proficient in ICT (Information and Communication Technologies), self-reliant, highly socially adept, capable of adapting easily to work environments, and able to collaborate with anyone, anywhere, and at any time.

However, even though today's children may not know what the future holds for them, it is evident that they must possess the necessary

resources to adapt to whatever comes their way.

Some experts in the field of education envision the paths to progress. For instance, as stated by Richard Gerver, former headteacher of Grange Primary School in Britain, creativity creates opportunities for talent to flourish. However, today's education system stifles that creativity. So, as parents, how can we encourage and challenge our children to boost their creativity? Students are born creative, and both the educational system and parents need to create conditions for children and adolescents to fully develop their minds and creative expression.

Another avenue involves teaching our children or students about social inclusion. This is a significant axis in establishing public policies in a country for its proper development and sustainable functioning, where one of the cornerstones of this construction is today's children and adolescents, who will become tomorrow's adults.

Digital culture has been ingrained in the world and, of course, in society for years. Educational institutions and families cannot remain detached from this reality. That's why it's crucial to have institutional and family leadership grounded in building a strong sense of community, combined with the use of ICT (Information and Communication Technologies) for pedagogical purposes, both inside and outside the home. Essentially, it's about uniting forces to teach responsible and critical use of new technologies. These can be incredibly useful tools if we teach how to use them with discernment and responsibility, thereby fostering emotional maturity, empowerment, and the healthy development of a child's or adolescent's personality.

Education and Subjectivity

*"Subjectivity is influenced by the historical modes of
representation through which each society determines
what it deems necessary for the formation of
individuals capable of unfolding within its midst."*
S. Bleichmar, *2005.*

An education focused on the learners, that is, children, adolescents, and the social and individual differences they present within specific social contexts, is a more efficient and comprehensive education. Its main objective is to understand and comprehend the psychological characteristics of these individuals and the cultural expressions linked to

114

the shaping of their subjectivity. Addressing the challenges posed by socialization and primary education in today's context is another significant challenge of contemporary education.

A Subject Existing Within the Educational Relationship? There is no pre-existing subject, but rather a subject *OF* and *IN* the educational situation. Studied by developmental psychology and, in general, by educational sciences.

Each subject is an infinite multiplicity, whose subjectification depends on certain circumstances: one is a subject in a situation and of the situation.

This implies taking seriously the productive nature of the *school system*, as it is in this system that processes of subjective constitution take place, as well as within the *family structure* and *society* at large.

When we talk about subjectivity, from the Latin *'subiectivus,'* that which belongs to the subject, establishing an opposition to the external; it refers to a certain way of feeling and thinking that is inherent to the subject. It is a psychological, chronological, and logical process through which a subject becomes one, from the earliest years of life.

From a philosophical standpoint, it refers to the specific interpretations that discern any aspect of experience. From a psychological perspective, these interpretations are unique to the person experiencing them; they are subjective qualities of mental experiences and are accessible only to the consciousness of that individual. Even though certain parts of the experience are objective and accessible to anyone, others are solely products of the individual themselves.

Numerous variables influence the formation of an individual's subjectivity, such as species, culture, historical context, the social group a human is a part of, and the traits and characteristics of each individual.

Taking into account factors like culture or historical context in which a human exists helps us understand not only their subjectivity but also how to educate them more effectively. Regarding mandatory education, for example, in our culture, it has not always existed, nor has it had a consistent duration or degree of universality. The same applies to adolescence, whose temporal boundaries and psychological characteristics are closely related to the ease of accessing adult status: economic independence tied to stable integration into the job market, forming a separate family from the family of origin, emotional independence, leaving the childhood home, etc. And to offer another example, retirement has not always been a reality in our culture, nor has it always been fixed at the same age. This is why, for developmental processes in which the role of culture is important, it's also crucial to understand the level of dynamism within that culture and the historical moment in which development is occurring. We cannot claim that all children and adolescents belonging to the same culture and living in a specific historical moment will have similar developmental processes.

For instance, the diversity of vocabulary, syntactic complexity, and semantic richness of the language that is learned are largely conditioned by the language spoken in the child's family environment. We are born distinct and then live from the beginning through different experiences that exert their impact on our developmental process, causing our psychological profiles to become more markedly individual as we move away from the starting point of our development.

At this level of analysis, psychological development or the formation of subjectivity, as shown in the diagram, occurs at a crossroads of influences where individual traits are not lost, but they are far from being the only factors to consider if we want to understand why psychological and educational development unfolds in a certain way in a human being – our subject of current education.

Concept of the Human Being and Integral Education

We define the human being as a bio-psycho-socio-spiritual unity. In other words, composed of its dimensions: biological, psychological, social, and spiritual. We can also say that, from an integral perspective, it consists of three components: body, soul, and spirit. (See 1 Thessalonians 4:23 "And may the God of peace Himself sanctify you completely, and may your whole spirit, soul, and body be preserved blameless...").

When we speak of these three dimensions that constitute the human being, from this integral conception, we identify that the body refers to matter, the tangible, the visible, the finite, and that which occupies a specific place and space. It allows us to relate horizontally, with creation and other human beings, in the order of the natural.

Soul or Psyche is composed of thoughts, emotions, and internal will or motivation. (See Proverbs 4:23 "Above all else, guard your heart, for everything you do flows from it." In the original text, the word "heart"

116

refers to the seat or place where a person's intellect, emotions, and will are housed). It refers to what is essential, intangible, invisible, abstract, eternal, and immaterial. It allows us to relate horizontally, with greater depth, to creation and other human beings, in the order of the natural. The word "soul" is the Hebrew word "nephesh" and the Greek word "psuche."

Spirit also refers to what is essential, intangible, invisible, abstract, eternal, and immaterial. It allows us to relate to the reality that is beyond the natural order – the supernatural. With the deity of God. The word "spirit" is "ruaj" in Hebrew and "pneuma" in Greek. It's important to distinguish that we're not talking about religion here, but about relating to God through faith, in the spiritual realm, not the material. It's necessary for the human being to possess spirit in order to connect and experience the spiritual realm. That's why it's said, "The spiritual accommodates to the spiritual."

The concept of religion derives from "re-ligare," which refers to the human attempt to reconnect or bind with God. Therefore, it's constructed by a set of customs, beliefs, norms, values, procedures that a particular religion deems necessary to establish a connection with God. Each human who enters the realm of that religion and wishes to be part of it must comply, practice, and adhere to this set of elements that the religion presents. On the other hand, when we refer to the human spirit and its relationship with the transcendent or spiritual world and with the Deity of God, we speak in terms of connecting through Faith, which is an entirely immaterial, spiritual, and abstract aspect necessary to link with God. Regardless of religion, faith presents to the human being the opportunity to experience a relationship of well-being with their Creator. It avoids falling into religious fanaticism, which can arise from the path of religion.

Considering all of the above, education will be integral if it aims and focuses on the holistic development of the child or adolescent. Consequently, it will be truly effective education that produces significant and profound transformations.

It is an education that includes the development of emotional intelligence.

Let's start by defining- what is an emotion?

Emotions are the existential compass that indicates the unique path of each individual, as they constitute authentic signals of who we are and who we want to be. They are the root of every vocation, the substance of each passion, and the fuel that keeps us in action to achieve personal triumph. In this sense, as Fritz Perls (1997) argues, they are the force that energizes all our actions.

Emotion is a word whose etymological meaning comes from Latin and means motion, movement, impulse that leads to action. Therefore, emotions motivate action, they move us to satisfy our needs and achieve our desires.

An emotion is something that a person feels that makes them react in a certain way; this reflects the fact that emotions are experienced individually, as not all people feel or react in the same way. In this sense, Bisquerra (2000) explains that an emotion is "a complex state of the organism characterized by excitement or disturbance that predisposes to an organized response. Emotions are usually generated in response to an external or internal event".

Norberto Levy (2005) argues that we cover up unpleasant emotions believing that they are the problem when they are actually just a signal that indicates the problem. Emotions themselves are never the problem. They are only information that, when ignored, can transform into energy. And like a debt in a bank, if one does not take care of them, they can generate problems.

E. Bachrach (2013), a biologist specializing in creativity, argues that happiness increases the possibilities of having insights or experiences of creativity, while anxiety reduces them.

Emotions play a central role in social interactions, as well as in behavior in all environments. For example, in the classroom, both the teacher and the students experience various emotions: joy, anger, sadness, fear, shame, helplessness, satisfaction, boredom, among others. In other words, the flow of emotions is constant and reflects the internal world of students, as well as their emotional state and their disposition for learning.

Furthermore, many of the problems and difficulties in life result from making mistakes because we ignore how emotional life works. They often result from emotional illiteracy. That's why it's important to develop Emotional Intelligence.

What is Emotional Intelligence?

"Individuals who cannot bring a certain order to
their emotional lives engage in internal battles that
sabotage their ability to concentrate on work and
think clearly."
Daniel Goleman

The concept of emotional intelligence emerged in response to a seemingly simple question: Why do some people adapt better than others to the different contingencies of life?

Until the 1980s, intelligence was considered to be a set of essentially intellectual abilities – analytical, synthetic, reasoning, memory, etc. – with Intelligence Quotient (IQ) being its most widely accepted measure. However, early psychologists who scientifically studied this capacity, such as Thorndike and Wechsler, had already pointed out that there were likely non-intellectual factors linked to intelligent behavior.

Howard Gardner (1983), director of the Project Zero and professor of psychology and education sciences at Harvard University, introduced a relatively new perspective by stating that there is no global and all-encompassing intelligence, as proposed by Spearman. Instead, multiple intelligences coexist, and consequently, a person could be intelligent in different areas.

When discussing Multiple Intelligences, Gardner helped reclaim the concept of intelligence beyond the intellectual realm, paving the way for emotional intelligence. While psychologist Reuven Bar-On was the first to mention an Emotional Quotient parallel to the Intelligence Quotient in his doctoral thesis in 1988, two American psychologists, Dr. Peter Salovey and Dr. John Mayer (1997), coined the term Emotional Intelligence. Subsequently, through the work of Daniel Goleman (1995), the concept spread worldwide with his book "Emotional Intelligence".

Emotional Intelligence is conceived as a genuine form of intelligence based on the adaptive use of emotions so that an individual can solve problems and effectively adapt to their surroundings.

Emotional Intelligence entails the ability to perceive, assess, and express emotions accurately; the capacity to access and generate feelings to facilitate thinking; the aptitude to comprehend emotions and emotional knowledge; and the skill to regulate emotions that foster intellectual and emotional growth.

Emotional Intelligence can be enhanced over time through experience and the maturity gained throughout life, enabling individuals to examine and steer their emotions when similar situations arise.

In essence, Emotional Intelligence is a set of personal, emotional, and social skills and abilities associated with individuals' behavior. It has been defined as the capacity to recognize one's own feelings and the skill to manage them effectively in specific moments. Goleman (1995) defines it as the ability to recognize emotions in oneself and others, adeptly managing them when collaborating with others. He suggests that it is a feeling that affects one's own thoughts, psychological states, biological conditions, and will for action.

Emotional Intelligence Components

According to Goleman (1999), Emotional Intelligence is grounded in five basic competencies, divided into personal and social domains. Competency refers to a personality trait or a set of habits that lead to superior or more effective performance. These five competencies are: Self-awareness, Self-regulation, Motivation, Empathy, and Social Skills. The first three are categorized as personal competencies, while the last two are social competencies. Personal competencies are those that determine self-mastery, and social competencies are those that determine how individuals manage relationships with others and with society in general.

Self-awareness. This competency refers to knowing what one is feeling at any given moment and using those preferences to guide decision-making.

It involves recognizing feelings as they occur. This implies the ability to experience one's own emotions, being capable of identifying them, naming them, or symbolizing them—putting them into words. It means being conscious of our emotional state and our thoughts and ideas about that state, as thoughts and emotions are intimately connected.

Having a clear self-awareness and awareness of one's emotional processes is highly important because the emotional behavior model exhibited by teachers or parents becomes a determining event that influences the emotional learning of their children or students.

Self-regulation involves the ability to manage emotions in a way that enhances tasks rather than hinders them. It is the capacity to manage emotions and choose how to deal with them. This includes the skill of appropriately expressing emotions based on the circumstances, which means finding the right space, time, and manner to do so—selecting the assertive way of expressing feelings and acting in the most suitable and authentic manner possible.

Self-regulation can be taught and learned, and it should become a pedagogical objective in the sense that it involves taking responsibility, determining sequences of actions, and making predictions, all while being a necessary means to achieve personal autonomy.

Motivation or self-motivation. This involves using one's deepest preferences to guide and move towards goals.

This aptitude is also depicted as the productive utilization of emotions. The extent to which we can motivate ourselves greatly influences our chances of success in whatever we do. This motivation stems from harnessing the productive energy inherent in emotions, utilizing this boundless force by investing it in activities we enjoy or prefer. Moreover, self-motivation is closely connected to self-regulation, as it provides the strength to endure setbacks, get back up after falling, and persistently pursue long-term objectives.

As educators responsible for the task at hand, both teachers and parents need to not only convey the knowledge generated by science but also impart other valuable life lessons. These lessons might include learning to confront adversity, maintaining persistence in effort, and striving to achieve personal goals.

Empathy. It involves perceiving what others feel and being able to see things from their perspective.

Empathy is the term for the ability to recognize emotions in others. It originates from the Greek word "empatheia," which roughly translates to "feeling within," meaning perceiving what someone else feels inside themselves. Feelings often aren't expressed verbally but through tone of voice, gestures, looks, and so on. The key to empathy lies in the skill of interpreting body language.

This aptitude finds its roots in emotional self-awareness, as the more open we are to our own emotions, the more skilled we become in interpreting the emotions of others.

In relation to the above, actively perceiving students' emotions and feelings means understanding their motivations. At the same time, it implies showing them that as educators, teachers also acknowledge the emotional impact of their problems, the challenges they're facing, the sadness of failures, the joy of successes, rejection, etc. Tuning into students' feelings doesn't mean accepting or agreeing with them on everything; it simply means understanding them and being willing to assist within the bounds of one's capabilities and limitations.

<u>Social Skills</u>. It involves managing emotions effectively in interpersonal relationships and interpreting social situations and networks accurately.

This aptitude is also translated as the art of handling emotions in relationships with others, a skill that determines our capacity for interpersonal effectiveness.

The lack of social competence during school years is related to problematic behaviors such as school dropout, low academic performance, juvenile delinquency, and criminal conduct. Similarly, adequate social competence during school years is linked to good academic performance and a person's popularity within their environment. For instance, as Malaisi (2016) suggests, in schools, this can be observed in children who solve their peers' problems, take on the role of peacemaker or class leader.

Social skills encompass communication skills, charm or likability, charisma, and the ability to mediate and reach agreements. They also involve the ability to negotiate and resolve interpersonal conflicts.

Many teachers often wonder how to navigate successfully through critical and challenging situations they encounter in their educational tasks: the hostility of some students, parents, or colleagues, the stress and anxiety of preparing a new subject they are unfamiliar with, criticism from a superior about their classroom management, the apathy caused by repetitive tasks, among others. The strategies used by teachers to manage these emotionally charged situations can vary: avoiding, enduring, minimizing, altering events, or seeking information and advice.

In most cases, students might not feel confident enough to come and share their concerns; however, if teachers pay attention to their non-verbal emotional expressions, they will likely find symptoms or signals that warn of these concerns.

The ability to recognize these emotional signals and interpret them will be the first step to connect with them, to empathize; while indifference or an automatic and stereotypical response can create a barrier. Then, the task will be to listen to them, reducing their fears and creating a favorable climate for interpersonal communication. Once the teacher obtains enough firsthand information, they will be able to provide assistance and offer alternative solutions to their problems or difficulties.

The self-awareness and self-control abilities of teachers will be essential in these cases. The former to identify and recognize emotions in others, and the latter to avoid becoming blocked by their own and others' emotions.

Benefits of Emotional Intelligence

"Emotional intelligence is useful in times of prosperity, indispensable in times of crisis."
-Dr. Hendrie Weinsinger-

Why is it necessary to learn to reason, understand, and regulate our emotions in the educational context? The reason is that teaching is one of the professions with the highest risk of experiencing various illnesses. In brief, it is a reality that teachers nowadays increasingly experience a variety of disorders and symptoms related to anxiety, anger, depression, and the well-known burnout syndrome. These mental health problems are sometimes exacerbated by the appearance of various physiological alterations - e.g., ulcers, insomnia, tension headaches, among others - as a result of various stressors in the work environment that contribute to their onset and development.

Currently, teachers must face a different position, new challenges, and challenges that are quite different from those of previous decades. Aspects such as students' lack of discipline, behavioral problems, excessive class sizes, lack of motivation to learn, student apathy towards assigned school tasks, and low performance have become significant sources of stress for teachers that impact their work performance. That's why the development of emotional intelligence is highly relevant in education.

According to Goleman, emotional intelligence ranks second, just below intellectual intelligence, in determining outstanding job performance.

The analyses conducted by dozens of different experts, government agencies, and charitable organizations worldwide have independently reached remarkably similar conclusions. All conclusions point to the prominent role that emotional intelligence plays in work excellence, in any job.

A leader who can manage their moods is someone who also understands the mood of their subordinates.

Therefore, the great challenge is to understand the importance of developing a philosophy of healthy living and to take action with platforms that support well-being and happiness while repelling discomfort and illness. It is crucial to foster an education that stimulates and develops emotional health and personal satisfaction, resilience, frustration tolerance, and self-motivation, among other emotional resources and skills, both in teachers and students, as well as parents, through the educational institution and the family platform.

In recent decades, there has been a growing interest among educational professionals and parents in teaching social skills to students, skills that should become true competencies. This interest is primarily motivated by the results provided by various researchers, demonstrating that social incompetence or inability in childhood is associated with both current and future personal, social, and school maladjustment.

Hartup (1992) established that the best indicator in childhood for adaptation in adulthood is not school grades or classroom behavior, but the child's ability to relate to other children. Children who are generally not accepted by others, who are identified as aggressive or disruptive, who cannot maintain close relationships with other children and cannot fit into the culture to which their peers belong, are at serious risk.

It is important to keep in mind that possessing adequate Emotional Intelligence is essential and fundamental, considering it as the foundation for the development and implementation of effective behaviors.

A change in approach and attitudes is necessary in this regard, as schools and families can, and should, promote students' social competence and, consequently, develop mental health and prevent future emotional and social problems.

In summary, the specific effects of emotional education are numerous, leading to outcomes such as improved self-esteem and self-concept, which in turn affect the level of social skills and satisfactory interpersonal relationships, reduced antisocial or socially disordered behavior, decreased self-destructive thoughts, lower rates of violence and aggression, fewer class expulsions, lower risk of drug initiation, better school, social, and family adaptation, and improved academic performance, among others.

It is becoming increasingly evident that overall success and well-being in adulthood can be a consequence of early learning in the use of these social and emotional skills to productively navigate life changes, as they reduce the risk of mental health problems and enhance psychological well-being.

What does Emotional Education involve?

*"If we truly want to intervene effectively in the
emotional process, we must understand them well
enough to find the most appropriate remedy."*
Daniel Goleman

Emotional Education can be defined from various perspectives. One of them, considering its ultimate purpose, is related to an educational strategy for promoting health, aimed at improving people's quality of life through the development of emotional skills.

Emotional education is also defined as a continuous and ongoing educational process that aims to enhance the development of emotional competencies as an essential element of human development, with the purpose of equipping individuals for life and increasing personal and social well-being. This can be achieved in various ways, but generally, it is understood as a form of training in skills and competencies.

It involves the planned and systematic development of self-awareness, self-control, empathy, communication, and interpersonal skills. It has taken on a fundamental role and now needs to be integrated across educational programming and teaching practices. In this context, it is essential to train emotionally intelligent teachers who can meet the challenge of educating their students with democratic leadership. Through their experiences, they can teach students to recognize, control, and express their emotions respectfully and clearly. The classroom atmosphere, shaped by the teacher's actions, will have a definitive impact on students' learning.

Emotional education, understood as the planned and systematic development of educational programs that promote emotional intelligence, emerges as a consistent and appropriate response to the needs at hand. It is an essential complement to cognitive development and a fundamental tool in preventing social issues.

Given that the purpose of education is to cultivate emotionally competent children and adolescents - capable of recognizing and managing their emotions - and, consequently, of interacting with others in an appropriate and assertive manner, the concept of emotional education arises as a way to involve the educational process in achieving this goal.

This intervention, focused on emotional development and mediated through education, should no longer be confined to isolated activities, such as those carried out during advisory periods. Rather, it should be integrated into the educational process itself. It becomes a cross-cutting aspect of teaching practices, so it's not only tutors who are responsible for addressing emotional topics, but also all teachers who interact with students, and parents as well, within their homes.

As an example, the following are some of the objectives of emotional education: gaining a better understanding of one's own emotions; identifying the emotions of others; accurately labeling emotions; developing the ability to regulate one's own emotions; increasing the threshold of frustration tolerance; preventing the harmful effects of negative emotions; developing the ability to generate positive emotions; developing self-motivation skills; adopting a positive attitude towards life, among others.

Ultimately, emotional education should be integrated into various curriculum areas, as an educational style for teachers and parents, who should convey appropriate emotional models in the classroom and at home.

It is important to note, finally, that the goal of Emotional Education is not to address an individual's pathology, but to activate resources within them. It aims to anticipate problems, working with healthy individuals to keep them healthy, strengthening and promoting overall well-being in the population. Unlike strategies to combat illness, the development of skills that promote health is self-sustaining and endures over time.

The following graphic provides a better understanding of this concept:

Health Strategy	Level	Definition	Who performs it?
Health Promotion: Emotional Education.	Health Promotion.	Actions aimed at improving and sustaining the quality of life and health. Does not address pathology.	Psychologists conducting Emotional Education, trained Teachers and Educators, Media, Social Actors, and other multiplier agents. Parents.

However, to effectively develop Emotional Intelligence in children, youth, and adults, a systematic and sustained effort is necessary, addressing three fundamental pillars: Emotional Education of teachers, parents, and students, which are further elaborated below.

Teachers

This involves the development of emotional skills in educators, enabling them to learn how to manage their emotions and self-motivate, recognizing that they serve as role models for their students.

It is understandable that many teachers might feel overwhelmed by the demands of their teaching responsibilities and resist dedicating extra time to teaching another set of skills. However, the acquisition of emotional and social competencies is not a separate endeavor but becomes integrated into the fabric of school life.

This entails providing teaching staff with strategies for promoting emotional education through preventive, mediating, and intervening actions. It involves equipping teachers with the strategies, skills, resources, and knowledge to promote education about personal emotions, which will eventually have a positive impact on their students.

In the classroom, teachers and educators assign tasks of emotional and affective significance. Society and educational administrations are increasingly recognizing the need for a specific curriculum that develops emotional content. Teacher-student interactions provide an ideal socio-emotional space for emotional education through everyday activities such as discussing problems, exchanging opinions and advice, mediating in interpersonal conflicts among students, sharing anecdotes about how the teacher resolved similar problems to what the students are facing, or creating tasks that allow experiencing and learning about human emotions, like watching movies, reading poetry and stories, performing theatrical plays, among others.

The ultimate goal is that with practice, students will internalize these ways of dealing with and managing emotions in their daily lives. They will learn to recognize and understand the feelings of other students or teachers, empathize with their classmates' emotions, regulate their own stress and discomfort, and choose to resolve problems without resorting to violence. In essence, teaching students to prevent emotionally violent and maladjusted behaviors both inside and outside the classroom.

Teachers serve as adult role models for their students, not only in terms of knowledge but also as an ideal representation of how to perceive, reason, and react to life. Particularly in primary education, teachers assume a role akin to that of a parent and become an indispensable model of emotional intelligence for their students. Alongside the teaching of theoretical knowledge and civic values, teachers have an equally important role to shape and adjust the affective and emotional profile of their students in the classroom. In almost imperceptible ways, the teaching practice of any teacher involves activities such as:

- Providing emotional stimulation and promoting regulated expression of both positive and negative emotions, such as anger, envy, jealousy, and more.

- Creating environments through school tasks and group work dynamics that foster socio-emotional skills and interpersonal conflict resolution.

- Exposing students to experiences that can be addressed through emotional strategies.

- Teaching empathic skills by demonstrating to students how to pay attention, listen, and understand others' perspectives.

The development of emotional resources in the teacher should be the first step to undertake this educational change. An emotionally intelligent teacher should possess sufficient emotional resources that support the emotional development of their students. Through this, they establish a healthy and close bond with them, understand their emotional states, and teach them to recognize themselves and resolve daily conflicts in a conciliatory and peaceful manner.

For all these reasons, one of the central axes of emotional education is learning to recognize and identify the emotions we experience. To identify an emerging emotion, training is necessary to teach us to recognize its various signs: palpitations, general sensations, intuition, respiratory rhythm, body movements, gestures, tone of voice, among others.

Becoming emotionally intelligent teachers is certainly a challenge. It not only requires spaces and times for training and work, but also entails a commitment that goes beyond the professional realm, encompassing the emotional and personal plane. The teacher's inner world is in motion: they must grow as a person, get to know themselves, and confront their fears and conflicts. This experience, in some cases, could be perceived as threatening and be developed with distress, feeding resistance. Despite this, taking the first step is essential.

Parents

This implies the development of emotional skills and knowledge of keys for healthy parenting in parents and/or guardians of the student.

For this purpose, programs for the development of emotional skills need to be implemented in a regulated manner within the school system, in the form of training programs that allow for family involvement. The fundamental role of the family should not be forgotten in this whole process of Emotional Education.

Although the school is a suitable context for emotional education, we must not delegate the total responsibility to educational institutions, forgetting the crucial role that the family plays in the education of children and young people. Therefore, involving parents in the process is essential.

It is not possible to place the entire responsibility for the student's socio-affective development solely in the hands of teachers, especially when the family serves as a fundamental emotional model and forms the primary space for the child's socialization and emotional education. Teamwork is necessary—family, school, and professionals specialized in emotional training must work together. Moreover, even when educators are aware of the need to address emotional education in the classroom, in many instances, teachers lack proper training and sufficient resources to carry out this work. Their efforts often focus on moralizing dialogues to which students respond with a passive attitude. For this reason, parents and teachers should complement each other in these tasks and jointly provide opportunities to enhance the emotional profile of the student.

Although schools are advocated as the ideal place for the promotion of Emotional Intelligence, it's important to remember that the learning of emotional skills begins at home, and children enter the educational system with different emotional levels. For this reason, teachers are not only faced with teaching but, in many cases, with transforming the emotional abilities or deficiencies of their students. Consequently, it's increasingly necessary for parents to be able to support the development of their children's emotional competencies, not only to enhance student learning but also to promote their own personal well-being and professional performance in their tasks.

Working with families becomes essential, as it's beneficial to establish systems of information, coordination, and shared work between school and families regarding interpersonal behavior.

In conclusion, it's of utmost importance that parents can develop emotional skills, not only to provide comprehensive education to their children with better tools but also for their own personal benefit.

Students

Emotional education must be present from birth through early childhood, primary, secondary, and higher education, as well as throughout adulthood. In other words, adopting Emotional Education throughout the lifecycle is essential, and therefore, it should extend throughout one's entire life.

Emotional education for students is carried out through techniques, tools, and working methods to be applied with children and adolescents in the classroom as part of the curriculum and in a cross-cutting manner, as well as in the family setting.

Emotional skills can contribute to social and academic adaptation in various ways. First and foremost, they facilitate thinking. Schoolwork and intellectual development involve the ability to use and regulate emotions to facilitate thinking, increase concentration, control impulsive behavior, and perform under stressful conditions. It can also lead to an increase in intrinsic motivation for students to complete their schoolwork. One of the fundamental components of emotional intelligence included in most definitions is the ability to self-motivate. Current theories of motivation highlight the influence that setting different types of academic goals -

130

performance or achievement goals - has on generating different motivational patterns in students.

Emotional intelligence provides the foundation for the development of more elaborate competencies. Mayer and Salovey's (1997) model of emotional intelligence proposes a series of basic skills such as perception, assimilation, understanding, and emotional regulation. Once these skills are developed, individuals will be better prepared to acquire more complex competencies that are reflected in many cross-cutting programs for preventing drug use, sexual education, moral and civic education, among others. For example, developing the basic skill of recognizing emotions in others helps foster specific competencies to effectively resolve an imminent conflict with another classmate.

In summary, teaching social skills is a clear competence and responsibility of the educational institution. On the other hand, developing our emotional understanding can help us, for example, understand the difficulties and sacrifices that often come with achieving a goal - like passing an academic course - and grasp the positive consequences that can arise from pursuing a challenging goal in the medium term - like attaining something promised in the summer; being able to choose the desired professional module.

Finally, those students who can regulate their negative emotions and maintain positive ones will find it easier to develop more sophisticated competencies related to frustration tolerance or assertiveness - like accepting criticism, defending their position non-aggressively, etc.

Furthermore, children who have deficits or problems in their social skills do not acquire social competence solely through exposure to the behavior of their socially adept peers. Direct, deliberate, and systematic intervention is needed for this to occur. To achieve this competence, social skills need to have their own schedule, be planned, and evaluated just like other curriculum areas. This is why there is an insistence on including the teaching and promotion of social skills within the curriculum, both in school and in coordination with the family.

All social actors can benefit from systematic programs aimed at promoting Emotional Intelligence.

Law of Emotional Education

"The pursuit of a more humane life must begin with education."
– Sabato –

In Argentina, there is a Bill of Emotional Education that aims to develop, through formal education, each of the skills of emotional intelligence, as well as the choice skills in each child and their caregivers – teachers and parents – through Emotional Education, with the goal of achieving a better quality of life for all citizens. This law promotes comprehensive education and seeks to enhance the learning and development of a holistic formation process for families and communities.

The World Health Organization (WHO) proposed the development of Life Skills in 1986. In 1993, it created a new document focused on Education, defining these skills as the abilities to adopt adaptive and positive behaviors that enable individuals to effectively address the demands and challenges of everyday life. Subsequently, in 1998, in the Glossary of Health Promotion, the need to develop ten life skills in the educational context was specified, of which at least six are emotional skills specifically[4].

For all these reasons, it is necessary to promote an education that stimulates and develops emotional health and personal satisfaction, resilience, tolerance to frustration, and self-motivation, among other emotional resources and skills.

---

[4] Correct, those are the ten life skills proposed by the World Health Organization (WHO):

1. Decision-making skills

2. Problem-solving skills

3. Creative thinking ability

4. Critical thinking ability

5. Effective communication skills

6. Interpersonal relationship skills

7. Self-awareness

8. Empathy

9. Emotional management skills

10. Stress management skills

CONCLUSION

Teaching the mind and the heart is the new challenge for families, schools, and the media, supported by public policies. As long as our children and youth continue to be victims of violence, whether they participate in it or not, adults remain responsible for the extent to which this contagious disease spreads – the most dangerous one of the 21st century.

This doesn't mean that Emotional Intelligence will drastically change our lives starting today. We must be realistic; these skills won't make us invulnerable or prevent us from feeling perplexed. Our emotional intelligence won't ensure that our students are well-mannered and motivated to learn, that our colleagues or parents of students won't disagree with us, or that our bureaucratic and administrative problems in the school will disappear. However, these skills will provide us with the tools to face reality from a different perspective.

Our societies require the promotion of Emotional Intelligence development, as it deeply affects the ability of children, young people, and adults to listen, communicate, concentrate, recognize, understand, cooperate, self-regulate their emotions, motivate themselves, and resolve conflicts adaptively, thereby establishing their chances of success and happiness. These are skills that support the development of healthy self-esteem in each person, and they are undoubtedly essential for life. It involves a change within each citizen, by promoting spaces to explore oneself internally and learn these skills.

If we desire a healthier, kinder, and safer world, then we must work hand in hand, as a team, uniting strengths, abilities, and talents to eliminate more and more of the obstacles hindering change.

There is no other path but that of integrating emotions. When managed well, they become a compass guiding us on our journey and providing the energy to navigate it. Conversely, if we ignore emotions, we not only forfeit the privilege of becoming aware of our existence, but also expose ourselves to great harm. That is not the way..

Thinking about Emotional Intelligence and its benefits allows us to realize that, to choose health in body, mind, and spirit, and peace in the world, we must integrate emotions. They are vital teachings that deserve their time and space in the formal education of every individual.

Chapter 10

CARE FOR THE SOUL

Ariel Gutierrez

*"… and she went and sat opposite him, a good way off,
about the distance of a bowshot, for she said, 'Let me
not look on the death of the child.' And as she sat
opposite him, the child lifted up his voice and wept.
And God heard the voice of the boy, and the angel of
God called to Hagar from heaven and said to her,
'What troubles you, Hagar? Fear not, for God has
heard the voice of the boy where he is. Up! Lift up the
boy, and hold him fast with your hand, for I will make
him into a great nation…" Genesis 21:16-21*

Once, in ancient times, a mother was desperate. She had a child, and they were in danger within the context of an unjust situation. In the midst of this situation, someone intervened to change the destiny of that child: God.

Every child is born by the will of God. This is a fundamental principle regardless of the circumstances that surrounded the event of their birth: an unexpected birth, attempts of abortion, violence during pregnancy, and various negative experiences throughout life's development.

"You formed my inward parts; you knitted me together in my mother's womb. I praise you, for I am fearfully and wonderfully made. Wonderful are your works; my soul knows it very well", states Psalms 139:13-14.

These are hopeful words that provide the foundation to affirm, based on the testimony of Biblical Scriptures, that God has a purpose for each person even before their birth, and that there is always an opportunity for healing and complete restoration at every stage of life.

When the adult world surrounding a child or adolescent is in turmoil, personal, social, and intrafamilial relationships, as well as interactions with institutions, become strained. Basic needs like love, respect, participation, security, a sense of importance, and discipline among others are neglected. The absence of this emotional support can lead to an insecure, depersonalized, aggressive, hyperactive, emotionally disturbed, substance-addicted, or poorly habituated adolescent or young adult who struggles to form relationships, among other challenges.

The soul is the part of our being that encompasses components such as the mind, will, intellect, feelings, and emotions. When someone's sense of importance, self-esteem, and value has been undermined since childhood, the entire system of the soul becomes sick and distressed, giving rise to negativity and wrongdoing in spiritual terms. This is where the understanding comes from the Word of God, in the Bible, that there is a divine work of inner healing to be accomplished.

God made everything beautiful in its time, and He placed in the human mind the concept of time, even though man cannot fully grasp the work that God does from beginning to end. Ecclesiastes 3:11.

Below, we can observe a simple yet inspiring diagram to contemplate God's intervention at each stage of life:

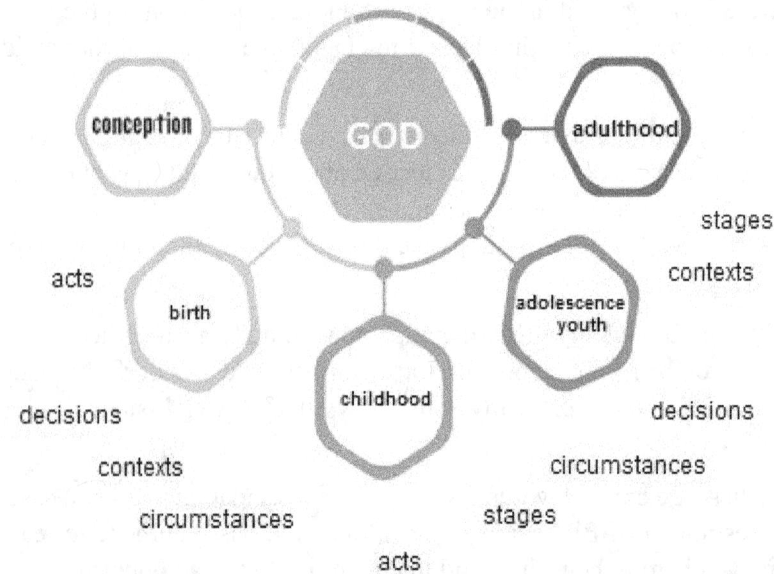

In this diagram, you can see a timeline with God placed upon it, for He is Eternal. For God, there is no past, present, or future. He sees us in a continuous present, which means His intervention at any stage of our lives will heal our entire life's history. While circumstances cannot be historically erased, the power of their memories can be, which may be hindering growth and maturity in the present and the future. This is the theological and spiritual certainty we have as Christians.

Experiences of rejection, neglect, lack of love, different forms of violence, and abuse shape a frightened, angry, and insecure child, who will persist in time, dwelling within an adult who hasn't been healed. Thus, along with growth and life stages, issues such as low self-esteem, insecurity, fears, personality complications, and even psychological disorders may arise.

However, there is an original divine plan that must be fulfilled, and that wounded inner child, scared, ashamed, angry, and mistreated, can be healed, for we believe in the restoration promised by God.

A significant number of young people aged 15 to 30 experience this healing. Some of these real cases, presented below with fictional names, will serve as clear examples of this healing. These are children who were not heard in their time or were denied the opportunity to have a space of attention in their family or in a childhood/adolescence consultation.

Carla was a young woman who couldn't establish loving relationships, even in terms of friendships. She carried the fear of trusting others, of opening her heart, of having lasting friendships or a meaningful romantic relationship. Added to all this, she witnessed her parents' fights that escalated to the point where she heard her father threaten to commit suicide multiple times. Eventually, her father left the house and became an alcoholic. The image of her broken father, devoid of commitment to his family, left her feeling insecure in various areas and unable to finish anything she started: courses, personal commitments, and work-related tasks. Once she overcame the traumatic power of these memories, she was able to complete her studies, pursue her projects, and even enter into a beautiful romantic relationship.

Joel, around 22 years old, due to experiences of abuse and violence in his family environment, struggled with a strong attachment to pornography. He was filled with anxiety and had low self-esteem. Today, he is in a process of overcoming these challenges and has already experienced some personal victories in his private life and interactions with others.

Once, as a counselor for children and adolescents, I had the opportunity to help Manu, an 11-year-old boy whose face exuded fear and shyness. One morning, unexpectedly, he burst into tears in the middle of his class. This boy was suffering due to his parents' separation and his efforts to please both of them every weekend. However, the core of his pain lay in the fact that both parents were absorbed in their own crises and new lives. Ultimately, he didn't have the attention of either of them. In cases like these, a pastoral counselor is there to help the child value themselves, find security in God, and discover a space where they are loved and appreciated. I also tried to contact his mother, with whom Manu lived, and guide her to focus on the situation correctly, in order to avoid burdening her son with the weight of her feelings of marital failure.

The result was a teenager and then a young man who was strong, resilient, and confident to face life's challenges. Over time, I could see a young man with a more open attitude, less fear, and greater happiness.

The difference in all these cases is made by the reality and spiritual conviction that God has a special interest in their lives and that they were born according to His will. That God is a Father who listens, who doesn't change, and who never abandons. And that they can fully trust in His presence and guidance in their lives.

German, around 24 years old, was a typical case among several young men: a deceased or missing father due to reasons that are never fully explained. In this case, the added challenge was that he didn't even know where his father might be buried. The lack of such crucial information creates a void in personal history that also hinders emotions, relationships, commitments, and the personal relationship with God. When the location of that grave was finally discovered, along with the story of his father, the victory of this young man translated into a marriage that recently began expecting their first baby. As the Bible says in James 1:17, "Every good gift and every perfect gift is from above, coming down from the Father of lights, with whom there is no variation or shadow due to change." And as Jesus said in Luke 8:17:

> *"For nothing is hidden that will not be made manifest, nor is anything secret that will not be known and come to light."*

The Healing Role of Religious, Leaders and Educators

It is very important for religious leaders and educators to undertake the task of "observing" the various attitudes where children and adolescents show the crises they are experiencing internally. Is the child very quiet and shy, or extremely talkative and extroverted? Are there violent tendencies or a rebellious demeanor? How do they communicate with others (peers and adults)? How do they react to affection? Are there attempts to stand out? This shifts from attentive observation to intervention or addressing situations of crisis for children and adolescents and their families.

In the task of healing and restoration, there is a fundamental role on the part of adult leadership, which begins primarily with containment through non-judgmental listening, understanding, and support. This action of containment is not only directed towards the children and adolescents but also extends to the entire immediate family and the surrounding home environment.

If you carefully read the Gospel account of Luke, in chapters 1 and 2, this child Jesus who "increased in wisdom and in stature and in favor with God and man" (Luke 2:52) had an environment of adult containment. His aunt (Elizabeth) marveled at this pregnancy, blessed the mother, and prophesied great things about the unborn child. There were people known from the synagogue like Simeon and Anna, who spoke great words about the mission of this child and advised his mother. There was social recognition from working people in the village like the shepherds, and divine manifestations through angels. "Of course, he was Jesus," a family can say, "not my troublesome child, nephew, or grandchild who has behavioral problems, developmental delays, violent tendencies, hyperactivity, rebellion, and other issues." On this path of spiritual healing for children, we have encountered many who have been cursed by their environment, negatively labeled, seen with limited potential, and professionally assessed as lost to normal development.

Andy, around 6 or 7 years old, was the result of a couple who not only accidentally conceived him but also never formed a marriage or stable relationship between themselves; they eventually separated. The ongoing conflict between the parents persisted, revolving around custody and financial support for Andy. This child displayed problematic behavior wherever he went: fights, disdain towards others, disobedience, shouting, tantrums, and violence both at school and in church. Attempting to make him pay attention in class, engage in activities, or have a conversation with him was nearly impossible.

Amidst this situation, his mother was nervous and violent towards him, while his father only issued complaints and criticism. A psychopedagogical teacher in our group evaluated him (with the mother's permission) and projected a future with limited possibilities due to the deficit in the development of his personality and self-esteem. In response, the other teachers and this professional collectively prayed for him, seeking divine intervention.

If you are a leader or teacher, possessing spiritual understanding and love for children, you cannot allow a child to live in a context of violence. After weeks of intense prayer and with the mother's agreement, new attempts were made to talk to Andy. Slowly, amid some stubbornness and tantrums, he began to accept these conversations, through which he encountered the divine love of Jesus and worked through his anger, hatred, fears, and pride. Today, although there are still some crises to navigate, this adolescent and his parents have found peaceful coexistence. It was a team effort involving counselors, teachers, and willing parents.

The case of Tomas was similar, although the parents in question had been divorced for several years and maintained a tumultuous relationship marked by grievances, accusations, and ongoing disputes over financial matters. Tomi was a violent and surly boy, an angry child carrying significant burdens. His adult world was a continuous turmoil that strongly affected him. Dealing with his parents wasn't easy, but in the meantime, as we attempted to introduce him to Jesus for his healing, Tomi slowly began to value this counseling space for himself. Amid his capricious attitudes and thoughts, anger, and stubbornness, his personality began to reflect the beautiful values created by God within him (as Jesus said, 'for of such is the Kingdom of Heaven'). This resulted in a child who listened to and received the Word of God, a mother who gained a better understanding of her correct role as a Christian woman, and a non-Christian man who learned not to fight. In this process, the seed of God's Kingdom was planted with strong roots, and we know that someday it will bear its fruit.

Children and adolescents are also ensnared into assuming misguided roles, exposed to risky situations, and subjected to witnessing various forms of violence and scenarios of promiscuity within family and social environments. These situations can lead to a future adolescent or young adult riddled with fears, insecurities, feelings of failure and guilt, addictions, and pathologies. That's why it's extremely important that signs that 'something is not right' are identified during childhood and can be addressed through child and adolescent Christian counseling or psychology.

140

Federico, an 11-year-old, was also timely rescued from a potential future of promiscuity and sexual addiction by being able to express his astonishment upon encountering pornography on his father's cell phone.

Tobi, a 6-year-old boy who was able to break free from the burden of taking care of his mother due to fear that his father (an ex-husband with a history of violence) might harm her. Praying for his mother, asking God to protect and heal her, brings great relief to the young soul.

Timothy, a 15-year-old with a rebellious attitude, prone to hanging out with gangs, getting into trouble, and using drugs, among other things. This behavior stems from a time in his childhood when he assumed the role of the man of the house due to his father's absence in jail.

The healing and restoration of Matthias, a 17-year-old who witnessed his father abusing his mother. This young man endured significant pain and deep failures in his soul and life history. In addition to the necessary psychiatric and psychological care, he also received pastoral attention. This wounded, scared, and powerless child found strength and new life projects.

In many of these life situations, psychological and spiritual matters are intertwined. It's challenging to believe in and maintain a relationship with a Heavenly Father. Thoughts of self-limitation and resentment take root, and in many cases, entry into occult practices in various forms or habits, not only substance abuse but also self-harm, negative mindset, and suicidal fantasies.

Spiritual intervention is crucial, where with the assistance of counselors, the children and adolescents are guided to strengthen their connection with God through faith and reject all the negative elements that accumulate in their emotions and developing minds. Likewise, referring them to specialized child and adolescent psychologists is important to rule out pathologies or biases related to personality disorders.

The Healing Interview

It's paramount to begin by being well-informed and prepared. For someone like you, who might be a devoted reader of the Bible and sincerely led by God, these are basic premises for someone with a calling for this delicate task. Additionally, stay attentive to other sources of information that will enlighten you about the current issues faced by children and adolescents, much like the present book that addresses the most common topics in areas every adult should be acquainted with. Sometimes, children and adolescents pose difficult questions and challenges. There are various ways to express inner pain, but there are also strategies for silence, whether due to fear, shame, personal devaluation, mistrust, or simply the normalization of negative feelings and acquired habits. There are periods of crisis in the advised individual's life and family that the counselor should be well aware of.

Secondly, it's highly important to allocate a specific time and place to listen attentively, without prejudice. It's within this act of listening and the space provided that the valuing of the minor begins, along with the establishment of a bond of trust that enables progress in the healing process.

Thirdly, it's important to consider that every word, every gesture, every expression holds great significance and reveals an inner life. The wounded child lacks a voice; they struggle to articulate in words what they are experiencing, often echoing definitions heard from adults. This wounded child could be biologically aged between 6 to 10 years, an adolescent ranging from 12 to 18 years, or even a young adult. Through attentive listening and care, we can also assist them in redefining their experiences. Recently, a young person with Obsessive-Compulsive Disorder (OCD) asked me which hand was the right one to hold the Bible with. Certainly, the obsessive aspect requires professional attention, but beneath that, in attentive listening, one can uncover deeper issues such as a lack of minimal comforts for reading and studying, general disorder, family conflicts, insecurities, the need for guidance, and the need for affirmation. It's important to determine what they believe the Bible to be and whether they grasp the significance of God's Word and salvation.

The fourth step is to help them bring the situation to God. Using a verse, a story, or a biblical character, guided by the Holy Spirit, the children and adolescents can identify with and see God in the situation: a God who is close, paternal, real, and mighty. Pray together first for a complete surrender of their entire life to Jesus. Encourage them to become believers and followers of Jesus. Then, pray to God for the children and adolescents, addressing each issue in a concrete manner.

We know that if we want to live the abundant and victorious life that God desires for us, we must reject what is bad and embrace what is good (John 10:10, Colossians 3:8-10). Healing and liberation from the oppressed, anxious soul surrounded by the enemy's lies, filled with harmful thoughts and habits, involves confessing faith in Jesus, renouncing the bad things acquired by personal will, and rejecting those imposed by the environment. But what about in a child, in an adolescent? How will they understand this process? As I mentioned earlier, by providing an understandable explanation of the Bible tailored for that particular child or adolescent. The dynamic use of Bible stories that allow the child or adolescent to see themselves reflected in the story's theme. Then, praying together or leading a prayer to God that the counselor guides the advised child or adolescent through. This prayer should be objective, addressing each issue to release, reject, and ask God for forgiveness: 'I ask for forgiveness from Jesus for my anger, and I don't want it in me anymore'— and to anger, we say 'out in the Name of Jesus!' (And then the counselor prays:) 'Jesus, may that anger never return to Nico in Your Name, Jesus' (as an example).

The promises of freedom. We know that in order to live the abundant and victorious life God desires for us, we must reject what is harmful and embrace what is good (John 10:10, Colossians 3:8-10). Healing and liberation of the oppressed and anxious soul, besieged by the enemy's lies, filled with harmful thoughts and habits, involves confessing faith in Jesus, renouncing the bad things acquired by personal choice, and rejecting those imposed by the environment. But what about in a child, in an adolescent? How will they understand this process? As I mentioned earlier, through an understandable explanation of the Bible tailored for the children and adolescents. The dynamic use of Bible stories that allow the children and adolescents to see themselves reflected in the theme of the story. Then, praying together or leading a prayer to God that the counselor guides the advised children and adolescents through. This prayer should be objective, addressing each issue to release, reject, and ask God for forgiveness: 'I ask for forgiveness from Jesus for my anger, and I don't want it in me anymore'—and to anger, we say 'out in the Name of Jesus!' (And then the counselor prays:) 'Jesus, may that anger never return to Nico in Your Name' (for example, spiritual and emotional principles found in the Bible are applicable in this pastoral process with children and adolescents - John 8:32, 2 Corinthians 3:17).

An adolescent, unlike a child, not only has a certain life history but is also undergoing a process of change and forming judgments about their adult environment. In this regard, there are fundamental aspects to consider: availability, building trust, acceptance, and support. An adolescent sometimes lacks words like a child but possesses enough determination and emotions to decide one day to share everything they feel and are experiencing. This is where the leader, biblical teacher, and/or counselor need to be available, offering the trust of a friend so that they can confide in them, assured of their discretion and genuine relationship. This person should be open to receiving all kinds of expressions and concerns without judgment or shock. The aim is to provide support, affirmation, affection, and empowerment, in order to guide them towards understanding and spiritually deciding on their freedom and healing.

Once, in a class of adolescents, a 14-year-old boy began sharing a significant portion of his experiences, highlighting his feelings of loneliness, after a long time of silence. To the surprise of the teacher and everyone present, Luis opened up about his wounded heart. This became a significant opportunity to subsequently address his situation alongside his teacher (who had previously built trust with him), allowing them to have a conversation and release burdens to Jesus.

Healing for families

Every child and adolescent is a part of a family and its history. Therefore, it's incredibly important to take into account that, in addition to having the support of parents who provide their consent for the pastoral care of the minor (a requirement you must absolutely fulfill due to ethical considerations and to avoid any other potential issues), it's vital that the pastoral work of support and healing extends to them and all those living in the same household. Even if for some reason this cannot be fully carried out, at the very least, an interview with the parents or the responsible adult accompanying the minor is necessary to explain how and why these conversations will take place (often requested by the parents) and to attempt to emphasize the importance of parents or responsible adults receiving counseling as well, because they need it.

Every family has a dynamic of relationships, which can be healthy or riddled with negative patterns. Repetitive cycles of situations can lead to constant crises among family members. Discovering these cycles is a key step in identifying and addressing the root causes of tension and instability within a family. It's crucial to pay attention to the stories and experiences over time, as well as any religious and/or professional interventions during past crises.

Listening, offering support, getting to know the parents, siblings, and other immediate family members allows for a pastoral approach to the healing and restoration of the entire family. Remember that the child or adolescent drew your attention for personal care, and they carry not only their personal crisis but also reflect a crisis within the whole family environment.

Informed consent

This form must be signed by the mother or father of each child or adolescent, or by a relative or friend who brings them to counseling. The teachers must be aware of the adult who accompanies them and should have their personal information, including address and phone number. Cases of minors being abandoned in counseling sessions have occurred.

The authorization/consent should include, at a minimum, the details provided in this example form. It's advisable to have multiple copies of the form prepared at all times.

I .... ID.............. am the father/mother of.......................... ID ....
residing at.......................... Telephone .... I request and
authorize.................... (Name of Area Director of Children and Adolescents or
Representative) to conduct a free, non-professional spiritual interview, one-on-one,
with my child as their counselor/teacher, whom I have voluntarily requested. I have
been informed of the procedure and have had the opportunity to clarify my doubts,
and I am satisfied with the information provided. The interview will take place
on.......................on .... and I release the institution and its members
from any responsibility.

Signature and name of the parent

Signature and name of the interviewer

Moments and Places for a Healing Interview

Physical spaces are crucial, and each institution should have designated areas for this purpose. To conduct an interview with the child or their family, a location free from noise and foot traffic is essential: an office, a room, a classroom. Having a dedicated space speaks volumes about the importance attached to this service. It conveys a sense of belonging, security, and privacy. It becomes a meeting place that children and adolescents will value, and even adults will feel supported in. Additionally, it's highly advisable to showcase the space that will be used, to both the minors and their parents, and if feasible, ensure the room has a window, not entirely sealed.

Equipping yourself with materials that aid in dynamic counseling with children and adolescents is also important: paper, pencils, simple board games, small toys, and the like. You might want to keep a notebook to take notes for specific prayers and to track the progress of each situation. It's recommended to use the play-test method that is suitable for both children and adults, which helps establish better communication and understand the child's family and school connections (see www.psicologaana.com)

Each meeting should unfold in a comfortable manner, without disturbances, haste, or interruptions. It's a dedicated time for listening, offering support, providing advice, reading from the Bible, and guiding towards soul healing and restoration. This requires a sense of dedication and commitment. As the Apostle Paul taught us: 'Seek the best' (1 Corinthians 12:31, 2 Corinthians 8:21, 2 Timothy 2:15).

When you embark on this pastoral work, when you find yourself listening to things you never imagined hearing, when it seems that it's never enough, even though you've prayed and surrendered everything to God, and you've prayed over the children and their families for the promised healing, restoration, and freedom in the Name of Jesus: you will know that you did what you were meant to do, at the right moments and times designated by God. But you will also carry a sense of dissatisfaction, a certain restlessness, a feeling that something was lacking. It's in those moments that you will recall the words of the Apostle Paul and learn to trust in God's Grace and not burden yourself: 'And who is sufficient for these things?' (2 Corinthians 2:16). God will provide all resources, even the emotional ones, if this work is truly a calling from God for your life.

And then, as you see those individuals who passed through your pastoral care with different countenances, new spirits, and new perspectives on life (even though you know that there is still more to be done and received), you will understand that you have been the instrument of rescue used by God for those children, adolescents, and families.

Chapter 11

FAMILY

Ana Carballeda

*"Those who are good in their families are also good
citizens".*
Sophocles

Much is spoken about family, and these days rapid changes and
criteria emerge that were impossible to conceive of in the past.
Nevertheless, there is a common thread among them based on enduring
foundations.

What do we understand by family?

*Family is a group of people who live under the same
roof, organized into fixed roles (father, mother,
siblings, etc.), with blood ties or not, sharing a
common economic and social existence, bound
together by emotional bonds – WHO (World Health
Organization).*

Family is also defined as a union of individuals who share a lasting
life project, generating strong feelings of belonging to the group, involving
personal commitment among its members, and establishing intense
relationships of intimacy, reciprocity, and interdependence.

Family is the basic institution of human society. It can be regarded
as the primary unit of health, from biological, psychological, social, and
ecological viewpoints - Médicosfamiliares.com.

Definition of family according to the Royal Spanish Academy. Meanings

1. Group of related individuals living together.

2. Set of ancestors, descendants, collateral relatives, and in-laws of a lineage.

3. Children or offspring. (He's married but doesn't have a family.)

4. Group of individuals sharing a common condition, opinion, or tendency.

(The entire university community is grateful).

As we can see, beyond the characteristics that may vary depending on the time, beliefs, and circumstances, it is maintained that within a family, an affectionate bond that transcends should prevail, along with coexistence, support, and solidarity among its members.

The family in human history

The concept of family in ancient times was different from what it is today. Let's examine some aspects that characterized families in many ancient civilizations.

In a broad sense, the term referred to clans and tribes formed by groups of smaller families, each with their own kinships, but without tribal-level kinship ties.

Elderly men, respected figures, were the heads of these 'family-clans' and were responsible for public matters.

The family units that constituted these clans or tribes were largely patriarchal. Polygamy was generally accepted for men, and offspring were considered fundamental and essential, with women bearing the responsibility for fertility.

Physical punishment of children was normal, and education was primarily the responsibility of the father, or alternatively, a teacher. Inheritance was reserved for male children, and women only inherited if there was no male heir.

Women were under constant surveillance: first by their fathers and upon marriage, by their lord (husband), who essentially became the owner of the wife through the exchange of money with the father. In turn, the husband provided a 'dowry' to the husband (servants, gifts, and land). The woman took care of the hard work and acted as a slave in the marriage. In fact, etymologically, the word 'family' comes from the Latin 'familus,' which means 'servant who belongs to a master''.

After some transitions, marriage became a matter for the Roman Empire, which determined the rights and obligations of the spouses, especially concerning property and inheritance.

In this context, it's interesting to pay attention to the relationship between the terms 'marriage' and 'patrimony,' where it's clear that the mother (mater) was part of the partnership, but the father (pater) was responsible for the assets (even if they came from the woman).

Over time, the Catholic Church assumed control over sexuality, with its main purpose being, and continuing to be according to the institution, procreation.

Within the Christian sphere, based on the teachings of Jesus, the monogamous and indissoluble nature of marriage was established. Duties of children towards their parents (obedience and respect) and of parents towards their children (support, education, and correction) were prescribed.

Matriarchy was present in a few societies, such as those in the tropical rainforests of northwestern Amazonia and central Brazil, as well as in southwestern China.

Not all societies were monogamous (even today, Mormons in Utah, USA, practice male polygamy). Until the mid-20th century, it was common for men to have more than one wife. Fidelity was a requirement for women but not necessarily for men.

Kinship relationships were primarily maternal: the mother's identity was always known, but not necessarily the father's. This form of kinship is called matrilineage and should not be confused with matriarchy.

As society entered modernity, the family became a private space, which is related to the emergence of the concept of the "individual" and the centrality of the human being (Humanism). It's interesting to observe the privatization of the family space through legal mechanisms, social contracts, and so on.

The Industrial Revolution and increasing urbanization processes significantly transformed the family structure. The number of family members decreased, giving rise to the nuclear conjugal family.

Starting from the 20th century, the framework, roles, and patterns of the family have been evolving over the years, undergoing significant changes. In recent decades (Postmodernism), there has been a departure from the traditional family concept characterized by paternal and maternal authority and defined roles. Instead, the modern family has emerged with a more independent and flexible structure. Roles are interchangeable, and household responsibilities are shared between partners, as women are now part of the workforce outside the home, just like men.

Childhood has been revalued, and the child, who was previously oppressed and marginalized, has become the center of maternal attention and the household. The State establishes regulations for child care and parenting obligations, and children's rights are recognized.

Different Origins of Family

- By Consanguinity

The consanguineous family is one of the oldest forms of family organization. Its main characteristics are related to the blood ties that bind its members.

It is based on a biological relationship, formed by blood relatives such as parents, children, siblings, etc. Consanguinity is the primary basis of kinship.

As mentioned earlier, the line of consanguinity extends through the mother, who can inherently establish the certainty of the blood relationship. Paternity, on the other hand, is an act of faith that can only be proven through DNA testing.

- By affinity

In short, affinity kinship exists between a married person and the relatives of their spouse.

Affinity kinship arises from marriage and is limited to the spouse, who becomes connected to all the blood relatives of the other spouse. However, there is no relationship between the blood relatives of one spouse and those of the other.

Family can also be established by the affinity given by a recognized social bond (as is the case, for example, with the family of faith).

- By adoption

In full adoption, the adopted person acquires the same kinship as a biological child of the adopter, with all the relatives of the adopter.

Simple adoption only creates a kinship relationship between the adopted person and the adopter.

- By care and protection

Today, we also refer to "family" as the network where individuals learn to protect and care for one another, beyond even their kinship relationships.

Types of family

If something has changed in recent times, it is the composition of families. Social transformations have taken place at an accelerated pace. The truth is that different types of families have existed for a long time, but only in the last few decades have they come to light and been recognized.

Although there are many types of families today, the following are the most generally accepted.

- Marital Family

This is a family composed of two people who have legalized their union through civil marriage.

- Non-Marital Family

A family whose couple is in a de facto union without legal civil marriage. Until a few decades ago, this type of family did not enjoy all the rights of a marital family. Currently, the situation has changed and continues to change.

- Family of origin

This is the family where a person is born and from which they are raised. When this person forms a couple and a new family, they carry with them the culture of their family of origin. It's easy to imagine that when two individuals make up a new couple, it will be necessary to interrelate both cultures, which is not always easy. Playfully, we could see these difficulties in something as simple as "Don't take it the wrong way, but I like pasta the way my mom makes it".

- Nuclear Family

This is one of the predominant types of families today, although it's not an absolute majority. It consists of a father, mother, and children. It doesn't include other relatives but maintains the traditional basic structure.

- Standard Family

The standard family consists of a father, mother, and two children. Currently, it's undergoing change, and some now consider it to consist of only one child. This is due to the fact that in large industrialized societies, the desired number of children tends to decrease for couples, or even the number permitted by governments.

- Extended Family

This was the predominant type of family until a few decades ago. It included the father, mother, and children, as well as grandparents, uncles, cousins, etc. It wasn't uncommon for them to live together in the same space and function as a unit. There are still families of this style, but they are much less common. In some countries, economic difficulties have led to a resurgence of this type of family due to the need to share spaces to reduce expenses.

- Blended Family

This type of family occurs when two separated individuals with children form a new family unit. It's one of the most complex configurations, as it requires significant efforts to define and assume new roles. It becomes even more complicated when the new couple has their own children (yours, mine, and ours). Extra difficulties can arise from members of previous families, such as ex-spouses, ex-in-laws, etc.

- Single-Parent Family

This is a family consisting of only one of the spouses and their children. This type of family is growing in the present day. Although there are cases of fathers taking care of their children due to the mother's abandonment, the majority of these families are formed by women, often impoverished due to the inability to work properly because of the care that children require. This problem is accompanied by the fact that women generally receive lower wages than men for equal preparation and tasks.

- Homoparental Family

Overview

This is one of the most recent types of families. It refers to same-sex couples who adopt or conceive a child and form a stable family unit.

The Law No. 26,618 of Equal Marriage was passed in 2010, making Argentina the first country in Latin America and the tenth in the world to extend this right to all individuals.

Its enactment allows any couple of legal age to get married, regardless of their sex, sexual orientation, or gender identity. Heterosexual, gay, lesbian, bisexual, transvestite, transgender, and transsexual individuals can marry their partners.

Never before has homosexuality been as accepted in society as it is now. Equality and non-segregation are prevailing in today's reality in most cities.

However, we find different and polarized viewpoints on this issue, depending on the moral and religious beliefs of each person. This has led to voices against this openness as well.

For a as objective observation as possible of the topic, all scenarios should be taken into account with equal respect.

There is no verifiable evidence that homosexual orientation *per se* affects psychological functioning. However, it's worth noting that the social situations many lesbians and gays go through, such as being exposed to widely accepted prejudices and facing discrimination, often cause acute distress. This distress can also extend to their families of origin or the families they form.

Regarding the expansion of same-sex couples into families, according to updated information, statistics estimate that around 15% of same-sex couples worldwide have children, whether biological or adopted.

In Latin American countries, legal adoption by same-sex couples is allowed in Argentina, Mexico, Uruguay, Colombia, and Costa Rica[5].

What options do same-sex couples have for having children?

The growing trend towards legal approval of marriages between same-sex individuals and their legal recognition has led to the implementation of increasingly diverse methods of reproduction for these

---

[5] Data extracted from https://larepublica.pe/mundo/2023/05/31/adopcion-en-parejas-del-mismo-sexo-los-5-paises-donde-ya-es-legal-que-parejas-del-mismo-sexo-pueden-adoptar-en-latinoamerica-adopcion-derecho-lrtmc-2092004, May 31, 2023.

new couples.

Although the controversy is intense, science and culture have gradually been incorporating new options to realize a new family with same-sex parents.

Homosexual parenthood arises in two ways:

1) When one of the members of the same-sex couple has children from a previous heterosexual relationship.

2) When the same-sex couple agrees to have a child with another couple or person of the opposite sex.

Next, the ways in which this latter proposal for having a child in same-sex couples can be carried out are presented.

Adoption

The possibility of adoption for same-sex couples has been gaining ground in different countries, but only a few nations still enshrine this right. Adoption is the legal act by which a relationship of kinship is established between two individuals; in this case, between parents and children. If the adoption is full, it will have the same rights and responsibilities as a natural relationship. If the adoption is simple, the legal effects of the relationship are limited.

Artificial insemination

Artificial insemination is an assisted reproductive method in which sperm is artificially deposited (using ejaculation devices) in a woman's uterus, cervix, or fallopian tubes to induce fertilization and pregnancy.

In general terms, a lesbian couple can resort to sperm donation, and one of them can carry the embryo and subsequent fetus.

Two lesbian women can go to a sperm bank, and one or both of them can undergo the procedure. The child born through this procedure will be legally considered the child of that same-sex union. Fertilization can also take place "in vitro" and be implanted in the mother.

Egg donation

A lesbian couple can decide that one of them provides the egg for fertilization, and the other becomes the gestational mother.

The procedure involves stimulating the donor's ovaries to extract eggs, which are then subjected to in vitro fertilization. The resulting

156

embryo is then transferred to the uterus of the gestational mother, who carries the pregnancy to term.

The sperm donor remains anonymous..

Surrogacy

If the couple is composed of two men, they can turn to surrogacy, and one of the men donates sperm. The process, known as surrogacy or gestational surrogacy, is a fertility treatment that is permitted in some countries.

This option is primarily used by gay men. It involves creating an embryo through in vitro fertilization using donated eggs and the sperm of the father or fathers. The resulting embryo must be implanted in a surrogate gestational mother, meaning a woman who "rents" her womb to carry out the pregnancy.

This method is approved in very few countries around the world due to significant ethical and legal controversies it can generate[6].

Effects of Homosexual Parenthood on Children

Are there any substantial differences in psychological adjustment between children raised and educated by homosexual parents compared to those who have been raised in heterosexual parent families?

There is already a significant body of research on this topic, with many voices advocating for different perspectives.

Since the late 1970s, systematic reviews have been conducted on the children of gay and lesbian parents in major psychological and psychiatric journals (Patterson, 1992).

Voices in favor

In general terms, those advocating in favor argue that scientific evidence indicates that the parenting abilities of gay fathers and lesbian mothers do not statistically differ from those of heterosexual parents (Allen and Burell, 1996; Brewaeys and Hall, 1997; Goodman, Emery, and Haugaard, 1998; Patterson, 1992).

Regarding parental quality, gay and lesbian parents exercise their parenting functions of care, affection, and guidance in a statistically non-

---

[6] https://www.ehowenespanol.com/opciones-parejas-homosexuales-hijos-info_303974/

different manner from heterosexual parents.

They all point out that there are no differences between the children of homosexual couples and those of heterosexual couples.

Intrafamily processes and relationships are more important than family structure. In other words, for a child's healthy development, teaching values, the importance of communication with children, and emotional management are much more relevant than family structure.

Homosexuality in children of homosexual families occurs with the same frequency as in heterosexual families[7].

Voices against:

The voices opposing this perspective argue that:

The absence of the male figure has created difficulties for the male child to relate stably with women, and vice versa.

Homosexual parents often exhibit rejection toward heterosexuals, and this rejection is more pronounced if one of the members comes from a separation in a heterosexual relationship.

The gay community, in which a significant part of the child's life is spent, often conveys hatred and reproach for becoming heterosexual.

A study conducted by the University of Texas in 2012, led by researcher Mark Regenerus, claims that children of homosexual parents exhibit poorer social, emotional, and relational outcomes compared to children from "biologically intact families."

There are also other questions to be evaluated, many of which seem to lack definite answers.

1. Will they be bullied?

One of the concerns raised when questioning marriage equality is the fear that children from same-sex parent families may become targets of bullying in schools. The evidence varies in this regard. While some find no difference, others do observe higher rates of bullying among children from same-sex parent families..

2. Could they have more psychological issues?

----

[7] http://www.interpsiquis.com/2003/ secretaria@psiquiatria.com - University of Valencia https://blog.cognifit.com/es/hijos-familias-homoparentales-como-son... Website: January 26, 2018

There is a fear that children from same-sex parent families might experience more psychological issues. This is an area where conflicting results also come into play.

3.   Does it influence their sexual orientation and gender identity?

Another concern among those unconvinced about marriage equality is the notion that children from such families are more likely to be homosexual. Some studies (Bailey, Wolfe, & Mikach, 1995) indicate that 90% of the children identified as heterosexual, suggesting that the sexual orientation of their parents has little influence. However, other studies offer differing opinions.

4.   Do children need both a paternal and maternal figure?

It is a fact that in same-sex parent families, children are deprived of either a mother or a father.

Supporters of same-sex parent families argue that studies show no differences between homo- and hetero-parent families. Those who disagree point to studies that demonstrate the opposite.

Of course, it's also a fact that single-parent families face the same issue, without involving homosexuality.

5.   Are they at a higher risk of being victims of sexual abuse?

Another concern surrounding same-sex and homosexual families revolves around the fear that they may be more prone to sexual abuse, especially if both parents are men. However, there's no way to definitively determine the percentage of abused children in same-sex parent families versus heterosexual parent families. Nonetheless, data suggests that cases of abuse occur in both types of families.

Prevention and Management of Discrimination Against Children of Lesbians or Gays in Schools

These families often have to deal with stigma and discrimination, and the truth is that this has a negative impact on the child's mental and emotional well-being, often leading to behavioral problems.

Some studies show that in same-sex parent families, there's no difference in the incidence of bullying compared to heterosexual parent families. Those who bully others will always find a reason to discriminate and humiliate, whether it's because someone is overweight, wears glasses, or has homosexual parents.

However, it's also true that this is a vulnerable population prone to experiencing such behaviors.

The primary effort to eliminate these issues should focus on shaping society's mindset, providing information, and normalizing not only these types of families but all family forms that differ from the "traditional" family (with a mother and a father married and living together with the children under the same roof).

However, until the few strategies that are being implemented can have a massive impact on societal beliefs, it's essential to work within the family sphere, as stigma based on sexual orientation will continue to exist.

Fortunately, we can develop strategies to minimize the impact of discrimination against this community.

- Help them understand that all families are unique in their own way, and that every type of family should be respected.

- Foster their self-esteem and social skills, as a confident and resourceful child will be better equipped to handle situations of bullying or stigmatization.

- Encourage communication within the family unit. Not hiding their origins or other information is crucial. By creating a strong bond of affection, support, acceptance, and open communication, it will be much easier to identify instances of discrimination.

- Promote emotional expression in situations of discrimination. If a child has faced discrimination at school or has been bullied due to being part of a same-sex parent family, it's crucial to provide them with a safe space to express their feelings.

Some ongoing conclusions from studies

The results of conducted research indicate that children from lesbian mothers and gay fathers have good relationships with their peers and satisfactory relationships with adults of both sexes.

The emerging picture is that children of lesbian mothers have positive interactions with their peers, grandparents, and adult friends of their mothers, both men and women, heterosexual and homosexual.

In cases where fathers reject the lesbian identity of the mother, Huggins (1989) found that the self-esteem of the children was lower compared to cases where fathers had a neutral or positive attitude towards

160

the mother's sexual identity.

In short, based on the conducted research, the myth that children of lesbian or gay parents are at a higher risk of being sexually abused, rejected by their peers, or isolated solely within lesbian or gay communities seems to lack a foundation.

From the opposing viewpoint, it is argued that the gay lobby consistently suppresses any scientific information that doesn't highlight the advantages of homosexuals over heterosexuals.

They have managed to influence the American Psychiatric Association to dismiss heterosexual affirmation therapies while endorsing gay affirmation therapies. They use their media allies to discredit any scientific research that doesn't favor them and criticize those who express a critical view of homosexual "parenthood.

The majority of research on the impact of homosexual parenthood has been based on interviews with same-sex parents, which are convenience samples. These samples are biased towards including individuals with higher educational levels. What about those who are less educated or have a lower likelihood of being employed? They were not interviewed. Naturally, the children of these wealthier parents are more likely to do well.

Sociologist Mark Regenerus presents a second expanded research that shows that children raised in same-sex households fare worse in life than children from heterosexual households. Regenerus had been fiercely attacked by gay associations in his first study on the topic, legally challenged, and even suggested to his own university that they strip him of his title for professional misconduct, while mainstream media have ignored the findings of his studies.

Multiple studies already demonstrate that same-sex couples, especially lesbians, have high divorce rates when marriage is available and stay together for shorter periods. Hence, instability is a constant in households with same-sex parents.

However, many studies also assert that children of same-sex parents do as well, or even better, than children from intact heterosexual households. This assertion is massively incorrect according to a new, large, and comprehensive study published in the journal Social Science Research. It was authored by Mark Regenerus, an academic from the University of

Texas, and is titled "New Family Structures Study" (NFSS)[8].

Important to consider: after thorough investigation, it seems evident that there is a greater number of pro-homosexuality studies, which are presented more prominently and take the forefront. Studies opposing this perspective are fewer in number and are harder to come by.

Family life cycles

The family life cycle is an organizing concept that attempts to explain the sequential evolution of families and the transitional crises they go through based on the growth and development of their members.

We could say it describes the life journey that individuals undertake from birth to death in the form of predetermined stages.

Courtship/Engagement

Courtship or engagement is the period during which a new couple gets to know each other. Its existence is very important as it allows them to determine if the chosen person is potentially the right one, if they match expectations. It cannot be foretold whether this acquaintance will ultimately be successful, but skipping this stage or not dedicating enough time to it can contribute to less positive outcomes.

During courtship, it is relevant to consider that not only the two members of the couple are part of the relationship. The cultures of their families of origin and the styles of each family also play a role, as well as the influence of their members.

Marriage

This stage involves true and deep mutual understanding, arising from cohabitation and maximum intimacy.

The early days can be challenging, as it's necessary to create the new characteristics of the couple, formed from the combination of traits each member brings from their family of origin.

For a quicker resolution of difficulties, it's important for the couple to enjoy independence. "The married, want their own home" is based on

---

[8]   https://www.aciprensa.com/noticias/personas-criadas-por-gays-tienen-mas-problemas-revela-estudio/   https://es.catholic.net/op/articulos/62777/las-dificultades-que-enfrentan-los-ninos-criados-por-padres-homosexuales.html#modal

the principle found in the Bible: "Therefore a man shall leave his father and his mother and hold fast to his wife, and they shall become one flesh." This statement tells us about the need for support and connection that should exist between both spouses, one toward the other.

The Birth of Children

The birth of a child is considered a family milestone. In many cases, it serves the purpose of transforming a couple into a family. Hence the expression "they've started a family" or "they've just become a family."

The arrival of a child triggers a realignment of family roles. It allows the involvement of individuals who, up to that point, maintained more distance, such as parents and in-laws who are now grandparents. They can be necessary for help in the early moments or for participation born out of the bonds of love established with the baby.

Education

A child's entry into schooling implies the expansion of their childhood world. Up until that point, the child only knows the model received from their own family. Now they will be invited to play at friends' houses and will share other family styles.

These relationships will either reinforce their own family model or, over time, foster a critical evaluation of their personal family unit.

Midlife Marriage

During this stage, the couple becomes acutely aware of what they won't be able to achieve anymore. This realization leads to a sense of urgency to attain what is still considered attainable.

Typically, at this age, parents have adolescent children who often become strangers. "They changed our child" is a common parental complaint. This is because parents, who were the heroes of the story not too long ago, are mercilessly replaced by the new figures sought after by adolescents. Adolescents choose to remove the "d" from parents, and their new heroes are their peers, without the "d".

The teenager moves. They change their body, their interests, and their expectations. The teenager must metaphorically "kill" their parents in order to begin the process of individuation necessary for maturing and entering into youth and eventual adulthood. This situation puts parents in crisis, as they not only have to deal with their child's changes but also with the personal sacrifices of dreams that will no longer come to fruition.

Independence of Children or Second Weaning

Time passes, and eventually, the family restructures with a certain calmness. The once-adolescent, now a young adult, turns their attention to pursuing three objectives: work, a partner, and a career.

The stage of the "second weaning" takes shape, during which the young adult becomes independent from their parents, and usually, there is a departure from the family home. Paradoxically, as distance is established between parents and children, a reconciliation often occurs between them, and children learn to revalue their parents.

How parents navigate this stage depends on how they've built their partnership and their bond with the departing child. The "empty nest" can be either a source of distress or enjoyment.

Retirement

A few years later, the time for rest arrives for the parents, which doesn't necessarily imply inactivity. Nowadays, more than ever, there are active retirees.

These moments can offer an opportunity to engage in activities that were postponed during more demanding times, as retirement age often comes with remaining strength and acceptable health.

Death of one of the spouses

In the face of the death of one of the spouses, a situation of sorrow or liberation can arise, depending on the type of relationship the couple had, the health of the deceased and the survivor, and the possibility of forming a new blended family once the grieving period is overcome.

Marriage

Marriage demands time, construction, and communication. I once read a humorous quote that describes it: "*There are marriages that work well from the very beginning, like a perfectly fitting glove. Yes. Too bad it's usually the neighbor's marriage*".

If we analyze it, parents are destined to depart before their children, siblings leave to form their own families, and the same happens with their own offspring. What remains at the end of the journey, until death do them part, is the spouse. It's wise to continually build the partnership, to give it time, so that once each spouse is alone again, they don't find themselves

164

asking, "Who is this?"

This happens when we stop paying attention to our spouse, when we allow ourselves to spend too much time extinguishing life's fires, which are always there, always coming, always present and never asking for permission: paying bills, taking the kids to school, sorting out costumes for patriotic events... All activities that impose themselves with urgency and more often than not steal time from what's important. The other person becomes "part of the scenery." But we forget to talk, to look into our partner's eyes, to delve into their feelings and needs.

To keep the flame of marriage alive, let's consider the elements that provide aid and support to the institution of marriage, as this bond is strong and truly vital in a person's life.

Elements of Marriage Support:

Love

Love is an action. Actions are carried out, they are realized. They are volitional, meaning they depend on will. This implies that if I want to love, then I love.

Love is fundamental in a partnership, and its existence challenges each spouse, manifesting itself in solidarity towards the other, in patience, in kindness.

Love makes us see each other tenderly, enabling us to cover faults that without it would take precedence. *Love makes us accept our spouse as they are, not as we wish them to be.* This statement makes a huge difference.

I like to explain it with a simple but very clarifying illustration. My spouse is like a yogurt in the supermarket refrigerator. If I want to buy yogurt, I choose the one that best fits what I desire, but there's a high chance that it contains some element that I don't like. Perhaps a preservative, or a coloring, or a type of sweetener.

Well, before buying it, I'll evaluate whether to take it or not. What I can't do is take the yogurt without that element. It's in the yogurt. It's a part of it. I have the freedom not to buy it. To leave it on the chilled shelf. But I can't disintegrate it into parts and take only the ones I like. That doesn't mean I can't proceed, within my capabilities, to make the yogurt better. For example, I can call the company and convey my objections and desires.

But it's up to them to implement the change. It's their prerogative. The yogurt is as it is. *I know it before buying it, and I choose it.*

Returning to the partnership, I can work towards its improvement, but again: it's as it is, and I chose it. It would be selfish and unrealistic to try to mold it to my needs, pretending that it should stop being who it is.

Love makes us accept each other as we are, as we chose each other, without giving up on the work of mutual improvement. It's a commitment in freedom that is carried out every day, put into action every day, and gradually transforms the "I" and "you" into the "we".

Respect

When there is respect towards one's spouse, it's not just about accepting them as they are, but also demonstrating this acceptance. I make it palpable that for me, they exist just as they are, without demanding that they become who I want them to be.

This respect encompasses the polarity of experiencing the partnership as a unity, as "being one," while simultaneously accepting their individuality just as I accept my own, loving them as I love myself.

The presence of respect in a partnership opens up the broadest possibilities for living in harmony and serenity.

As a corollary, I like to say that I can respect without loving, but I can't love without respecting.

Communication

Paul Watzlawick was one of the main authors of the theory of human communication. He identified five communication axioms, but here we will discuss only the first, which states "one cannot not communicate."

In life, we are constantly communicating. We communicate through silence, words, shouts, and gentleness. What we cannot do is not communicate. We also communicate in marriage. The question is how we communicate. Allowing time for communication, doing it with the respect we've discussed earlier, choosing the right words and timing are the seasonings that flavor communication appropriately.

Let's communicate in a manner that befits us: without shouting, without violence. Let's communicate peacefully. There's an old proverb that we can find in the Bible that says: "A word aptly spoken is like apples of gold in settings of silver... ...at the right time." Let's communicate positively.

A great help is to communicate from "me" rather than from "you." It's much more likely that the other person will accept it more graciously if I say, "It really hurts me when you speak to me this way," rather than accusing, "You always speak badly to me." The first expression is true, but the second... We are not "always" and "never." We don't achieve "Very well, 10 out of 10. Congratulations, keep it up" in "sometimes." My dad used to tell me, "Never say never. Never say always. Don't use words that commit you." So, let's communicate, as God commands.

Economy

This topic might initially be seen as too materialistic to be considered fundamental in marriage. However, it is of vital importance. The "For richer, for poorer" sentiment of the early days can be put to the test when financial needs become more pressing.

Having a realistic and agreed-upon budget, being responsible with expenses, maintaining control over credit card usage all contribute to building a mature and lasting relationship.

A serious problem to avoid is turning money into a power dynamic. Marriage is a partnership at 50%. Abusing power due to money can create pain and vulnerability within the relationship, especially if one spouse is engaged in tasks known as "care work," which often go unpaid (childcare, household chores, etc.). Once again, respect acts as a mediator in addressing potential disparities in the value of roles within the economic context.

Sexual life

A fulfilling and vibrantly shared sexual life takes time. It is built upon mutual understanding. It is nurtured through trust and dialogue that enables each spouse to know what the other enjoys.

There's no manual for the "perfect sexual relationship." Each couple will learn about their preferences and share their desires with one another. This takes time, love, communication, and respect—all combined.

The incredible connection experienced with a stranger after a chance encounter, culminating in shared climax after just a few minutes of conversation, belongs in Hollywood movies. That "making love" doesn't involve much more than genital contact. But genitals don't love each other. Making love is precisely that: making love. It implies commitment, deep surrender, mutual understanding that goes far beyond the body. It encompasses the entirety of each person.

Moreover, that fulfilling and vibrant shared sexual life, the one that takes time to build, results in hormones that lead to well-being, relaxation, bodily satisfaction, and even emotional contentment. It's worth nurturing a splendid sexual life within marriage.

Shared Future Projects

A marriage, to be solid and united, must have shared projects. The first project to share is facilitating shared happiness, even if it sounds like a play on words.

Marriage seeks mutual well-being, shared assistance, support for one's spouse. All these are projects established when creating a partnership. The story of Adam and Eve is well-known. Adam was alone in Eden, and God created Eve so that he wouldn't be alone. He was given a companion with whom to build his future. "It is not good for the man to be alone" signifies the need for companionship and the building of projects with someone else.

Generating future projects is a good investment for a couple. But let's examine the meaning of the term "investment." It comes from the Latin "Nec" and "Octium," which translates to "neg-otium," or in other words, negation of leisure, something that is not leisure. It's not necessarily pleasure. But it is a necessity.

These projects don't always arise spontaneously. In many instances, they must be sought out. They become a sort of investment. They may even demand extra effort from one of the parties. For example, let's suppose the husband enjoys fishing. If the spouse notices that the partnership lacks motivation, that there isn't something that sparks the desire to spend time together, she can offer to join him on a fishing trip (even if it's not a very appealing activity to her and her participation is limited to making mate or preparing coffee).

Generating future project "investments" is important and positive for the well-being of the partnership. And we're not necessarily talking about projects that generate economic profit, but emotional profit.

Trust

Trust is also built within a partnership. Nowadays, this element is priceless. It holds value. It's truly difficult to find someone who deserves our trust. It must be handled delicately, with extreme care.

A few years ago, I had the opportunity to visit the Island of Murano in Italy. There, I witnessed the creation of Murano glass pieces, which are very expensive and incredibly beautiful.

The work done by the craftsmen is slow and detailed. One wrong move, and the glass shatters irreparably. To fix the piece, they have to start the entire process over again, adding the time it takes to return to square one before beginning anew. Sometimes, they even discard the piece instead of trying to salvage it.

That's how delicate trust is. One wrong step, and it shatters. It's so difficult to regain it. Let's take care of the trust in our partnership. Remember: there's no price that can buy it back.

Divorce

Divorce is a legal procedure that ends the marital bond and allows both individuals to regain their status as single individuals.

After the court judgment is made and recorded in writing, the divorce takes effect. The primary effect is the dissolution of the marital union. It signifies the termination of the marital bond through a court judgment.

The concept of divorce dates back to antiquity and originated from Roman Law. It was called "divortium" and pertained to the idea of marriage, being considered when there was a clear intention contrary to marital affection.

Considering the definitions of family that we have discussed, it goes without saying that this step should not be taken hastily, but rather as a last resort, after having attempted all alternative conflict resolution options within the partnership.

In religious communities, the concept of marriage being a lifelong commitment is paramount. They view a married couple as bound together until death separates them".

Stages Typically Traversed to Reach Divorce

Pre-Breakup Phase

Divorce doesn't come as a surprise. What can come as a surprise, at times, is the reason that originates it. However, divorce is evaluated, analyzed.

This time of analysis, of weighing whether yes or no, is the pre-breakup stage. These moments can be filled with a lot of pain and suffering, as there's no certainty about how to proceed, and often the process remains undisclosed, traversing it in solitude until a decision is reached.

Breakup

Once the pre-breakup stage is surpassed, if the decision arrived at is separation, the breakup of the couple occurs. Each of the spouses assumes a new stage in which they interrupt their shared life under the same roof.

The speed or slowness with which a legally significant divorce is carried out (later on, different types of divorces will be discussed) will depend on the reasons the couple has. Legal divorce might alternatively appear in the various stages described below.

Single-Parent Family

Previously, we've discussed what a single-parent family is. If the separated couple reaches an agreement, the child will spend time with each of their parents. It often happens that adapting to this new system becomes complex, especially when the child loses customs and activities they enjoyed before the breakup.

Courtship or Emergence of a New Partner

It's possible that one or both former spouses establish a new relationship. In some cases, the appearance of a third person might have been the trigger that led to the separation.

The child needs to adapt to this new system, which will take time and effort. The love of their parents, necessary understanding, and unconditional support will be the elements that help the child accept this new experience.

Time will determine the strength of the new relationship. That's why it's not advisable for the child to meet their father's/mother's new partner until there's confidence that it's a serious relationship.

On the part of the adult, they must ensure how the newcomer will behave towards the child, a situation that must be discussed and agreed upon before the introduction. The attitude of the new member will be of vital importance.

Decision to Re-Marriage

The final divorce might already be established, in progress, or being approached through a new serious relationship. What's common is that this stage involves overcoming many complex situations. At this point, it's expected that interfamily relationships have smoothed out rough edges or are working on this process, both with the child and the rest of the families.

Blended Family Formation

The new bond is established with an official status, bringing about new adjustments of roles in the family. Further in this writing, more details about the blended family will be discussed.

Emotional Divorce

Emotional divorce occurs when a couple goes through a separation in their emotional bond while living or sharing the same physical space. In other words, they might be sleeping in the same bed, preparing lunch in the same kitchen, or working in the same room, but their hearts no longer share a romantic relationship.

De Facto Divorce

De facto separation or divorce occurs when one or both members of a legally married couple choose, in practice, to permanently break cohabitation and thereby interrupt their shared life. This separation can occur for justified or unjustified reasons and leads to a series of legal consequences.

Generally, within legislation, the concept of de facto separation is not explicitly legally recognized.

Spouses should live in the same house unless, due to exceptional circumstances, they are compelled to maintain separate residences temporarily. They can be judicially relieved from the duty of cohabitation when it endangers the life, physical, psychological, or spiritual integrity of one or both of them or their children.

Legal Divorce or Separation

Legal divorce is a process that opens the way to dissolve a marriage and consequently allows the members to remarry whomever they wish.

Is There Divorce for Children?

Definitely not. Divorce is between the parents. Parents do not divorce their children. Abandoning the children by one parent after a marital divorce indicates emotional immaturity of the one who leaves. The children become innocent sufferers in the situation.

Children must be protected in this situation by both spouses. No matter the relationship the parents might have with each other, however disastrous it may be, anger, resentment, and frustration should be put aside when discussing matters concerning the children.

Children don't choose what they are going through. They probably don't want it. But they have no choice but to accept their parents' decision. Let's not add more pain to what they are already feeling.

Divorce is about the couple. Parents do not divorce their children.

The Tupac Amaru Syndrome

For children, parents are their support, their anchor. When the conflict between parents becomes unmanageable, in the chaos of the battle, they lose sight of the fact that there are children observing and suffering in the midst of it.

Helpless and abandoned, they witness their parents tearing each other apart, and they love both their parents equally. Faced with this struggle, they are left as hostages and experience what is known as the Túpac Amaru Syndrome.

Túpac Amaru was an indigenous leader from the 18th century. Captured and tortured by the Spanish, he died with four horses pulling at his limbs in an attempt to dismember him. (Note: as they failed with the horses, he was eventually quartered with axes in front of his wife).

Metaphorically, this is the situation to which a child is subjected when their emotions are "pulled" in a battle where everyone loses: the child loses, the parents lose, and other family members also lose if they get involved in this senselessness, such as grandparents, uncles, and cousins.

Sometimes, the fight goes even further, and the child is demanded to take sides, questioned about the other parent upon returning from visits, or blamed for the love they feel for the other parent.

Parents are a child's safety net of love. Or at least they should be. Let's consider the sometimes irreparable damage caused to a child when spouses let themselves be driven by selfishness and pettiness during a divorce.

172

Consequences of Divorce

Divorce never comes without a cost. Even for the one initiating it, there are high prices to be paid and suffering involved.

These consequences don't just affect the couple. They extend to the children, as previously explained, mainly to raise awareness that children don't choose the situation, but they are forced to face and process it, hopefully in the best possible way.

Former spouses face:

- Emotional losses
- Financial losses
- Loss of social status
- Loss of friends
- Loss of roots

Children share some of the aforementioned losses and add their own:

- Loss of cohabitation with one parent
- Changes in school, home, and economic status
- Feelings of abandonment
- Adaptation to blended families.

That's why there are questions to ask oneself before divorce:

- Have you truly done everything possible to save the marriage?
- Have you examined the reasons?
- What evidence do you have that divorce will solve your problems?
- Do you know if divorce resolved the problems for friends and family members who went through it?
- Are you aware that a high percentage of divorced individuals say they wouldn't divorce again if given a second chance?
- Are you aware that the vast majority of divorced individuals report suffering emotionally, even if they were the ones initiating the divorce?
- Are you aware that divorce is among the top five causes of distress?

That's why... there are golden rules to avoid divorce

Golden Rules:

Love is Volitional

On one occasion, a person who was considering divorce told me what their spiritual leader advised. When asked why he wanted a divorce, the man replied that he felt he no longer loved his wife. The listener responded with a smile, clarifying that the problem had an easy solution. When pressed to know the solution offered, the spiritual leader said, "You feel like you no longer love your wife. Then put the verb 'love' into action and love her.".

At first, my interlocutor thought his leader was joking, but gradually he came to understand what this meant. Love is an action. It depends on willpower. It's a volitional action. Just as one cooks, takes a shower, drives a car, one loves. *One chooses to love, and then, they love.* Love is not just a feeling. It can have feeling, of course. But it transcends feeling because loving is love in action.

Love never ceases to be

I love comparing love to a cycle. Just as there is the water cycle in nature, there is a love cycle in our nature. Love changes over time. Romantic love, full of eros in its beginnings, transforms to make way for companionship in advanced old age. But it still exists. It continues to exist. Love changes, adapts, but never ceases to be.

Divorce isn't the first solution

One of the problems contributing to the growth of divorce in our times is the attitude of adopting it as the first solution. We've already seen that divorce implies, inevitably, pain. It's wise to fight for the continuity of the couple, for the well-being of the spouses and the well-being of the children. Divorce is not only not the first solution. Divorce is the last one.

God continues with each divorcee

Personally, I believe in God. If you don't, give this point the significance you find appropriate. From a place of faith, I am certain that divorce is not the best path, that one should strive to improve and beautify the marriage because, as we've already pointed out, the breakdown of a couple brings anguish to all family members.

If, nonetheless, you decide on divorce, if no other solution to the problem is found and the crisis seems insurmountable, a point to consider that can help in the midst of the pain is to view God as present in the lives of all those involved, lovingly supporting them through the difficult journey ahead.

Let's not judge. Let's accompany

If our role is to somehow accompany those who are going through this process, let's step away from a place of judgment.

As human beings, we tend to evaluate situations instead of adopting a constructive perspective that helps us offer as objective assistance as possible, distancing ourselves from personal biases and criteria.

To accompany is to walk alongside, to match steps, and that's indeed what someone in need will appreciate: respect for their feelings and experiences, without adding more judgment than they likely already have to deal with.

To fail is not to not achieve the objective. To fail is to stop trying

Think for a moment about learning to ride a bike. It takes attempt after attempt and more than one scraped knee. Those who give up, who throw in the towel due to fear, mandates, or shame, don't learn and fail. Those who get back on and keep fighting despite the painful scrape and bruised ego, end up winning the battle.

The journey to achievement is never easy. The mistake is assuming that not reaching the goal in the first attempts marks and determines failure. In reality, effort, work, and persistence are required time and time again before "getting off the bike" and saying "this is not for me. It's all over here."

As long as pathological situations are not at play, metaphorically speaking, it doesn't matter how many times it takes us to reach the goal. As long as we keep getting back on the bike, we haven't failed. We will still be in the race.

Once again, the blended family

The blended family and the nuclear family are both families, and the goal is for love to build both of them. However, it helps to know the fundamental differences between them. This knowledge can aid in the building process by being aware and having realistic expectations of the situations that are present:

- The blended family comes after losses.
- The parent-child unit precedes the new couple.
- There is another parent in another household or in memory.
- Different customs exist among the members.
- Generally, children move from one parental home to another.
- The extended family expands.
- Relationships with the former spouse are maintained.
- The new couple has to create their own space with more children around.
- The new extended family can either hinder or benefit.
- Jealousy often arises in one or both former spouses.
- Differences in parenting approaches frequently lead to problems.

Considerations to avoid future problems

Previously, we discussed cycles and compared the natural water cycle to the cycle of love.

Now, let's establish another cycle: the cycle of human life within society. Humans were created to interact in pairs. Loneliness is not a good companion; it's loneliness. It offers little companionship.

Marriage is the ideal institution for human beings. While one can experience a state of well-being in solitude as long as vitality remains, with age advancing and energy dwindling, and the house being empty, there's a shared desire to have someone to look into their eyes and sit at the table with.

At the same time, this marriage extends into descendants. Offspring fulfill humans' desires for transcendence, and in normal relationships, they are considered a blessing, an inheritance, and a reason for joy and celebration.

It is a well-trodden field to talk about the family as the foundation of society, but it became well-trodden through being experienced as reality. Let's remember the beginning of this chapter when the history of the family spoke of "tribal families" or "clan families" that integrated nuclear families into extended groups that defended and cared for each other.

Every child born into society incorporates their values and culture, growing up to eventually integrate into a couple that will bear offspring... and so the cycle continues.

This cycle of humans in society allows the species to perpetuate itself and values to be sustained and evolved.

From the Endogamous Child to the Exogamous Youth

As the child grows and absorbs the family and societal culture surrounding them, they incorporate patterns of behavior and conduct that are common in their environment. They observe their parents' partnership dynamics and project their future in an endogamous way. This is where we often hear statements like "Mom/Dad, when I grow up, I'm going to marry you."

However, as the child becomes a young adult, they naturally move away from this endogamous sentiment and expand towards an exogamous one – the search for a partner outside of the family. This process solidifies the normalcy and healthiness of parent-child relationships, moving away from the concept of incest.

Systematic Education as Support for Children and Adolescents

Up until now, we've approached the family from an endogenous perspective. Now, let's broaden our view to see the family from an external standpoint.

We've previously discussed a portion of the family cycle – the child's entry into the school environment – and examined how the beginning of systematic education influences the expansion of a child's criteria, later as a teenager.

Now, let's explore how educational authorities can impact the family's internal dynamics, starting from the student.

Increasingly, the educational sphere finds itself in a position of responsibility and collaboration with the family. While in the past, the school's involvement primarily focused on conveying information to the child, today it fills gaps as vital as nutrition and upbringing, either supplementing or taking the place of family actions.

Teachers often step in to perform tasks that should ideally occur within the home, contributing to students' formation rather than just information.

This situation, stemming from social circumstances that won't be examined in this brief overview, compels teachers and other school authorities to possess a training that goes beyond academics.

Below, we'll briefly introduce some elements to consider when assisting students with emotional needs stemming from family issues.

Guide for Teachers: How to Support Problematic Processes in an Educational Setting

Listen, listen, listen!

Think about it seriously: how many arms do you have, how many hands, how many legs, how many lungs, how many ears, and *how many mouths? Why is that?* It seems like we're equipped to listen twice as much as we talk.

And I dare to say that we don't have just two ears. In reality, when we accompany with deep listening, we have three ears: the two on our head and the one in our heart.

It's important to listen deeply with the three ears that humans possess. Keep your attention on what is being said, without succumbing to distractions or letting your mind wander, as that would be disrespectful to the speaker.

Listen to Understand, Never to Judge

If a child or adolescent has managed to break through the barrier of silence, they need to be heard without receiving criticism or judgment. You don't have to share what you hear, and you'll have time to help identify misunderstandings or actions in a loving and supportive way, but judging is fundamentally different. A person who feels judged will close their heart and their capacity for change.

You don't need to say much

In many instances, "the greatest help" is simply listening. Speaking can provide relief to the heart. Don't speak just for the sake of it. If you don't know what to say, the best thing you can do is say nothing. Silence accompanies more than empty words.

Recognize Our Limits

It's possible that a situation might exceed our ability to handle it. If a problem is beyond our scope, it's responsible to acknowledge it and refer it to someone more knowledgeable in that area. If the issue presented is too complex, don't rush into offering a random solution; take time to reflect on the situation and find a relevant solution, seeking alternative perspectives from others to consider.

Look into the Eyes of the Person You're Listening to

Ensure that you're giving them your full attention. Listen deeply without simultaneously preparing a potential response. Let the other person finish their thoughts *without interrupting.*

Avoid Making Assumptions

Humans tend to jump ahead of the other person's thoughts by drawing conclusions that can be mistaken or hasty. Allow the child or adolescent to finish speaking.

Never Dismiss the Person

Understand that what the child or adolescent is saying reflects their experience. Accept and recognize that what they're expressing is what they genuinely feel, regardless of whether it aligns with your own feelings.

The Problem of the Child or Adolescent is <u>the Problem</u>

Don't evaluate it based on your own criteria. If it's a problem for them, it should be a problem for you. Don't downplay it or compare it.

Ensure the Confidentiality of What is Shared

When someone opens their heart and speaks, they trust that their confidence won't be betrayed. Be respectful of those feelings.

Let's defend the family. It's the container, the support, the security, and the model that provides us with the best place of shelter and support. It remains ready to receive the member who comes in distress and closes ranks when the situation threatens.

The Rights of the Child

As discussed earlier in the history of the family, society established norms for the care of children. UNICEF commissioned the Argentine cartoonist Quino to put the principles of children's rights in the mouths of the characters from Mafalda, an emblem of critical freedom.

AUTHORS

Ana G. Kelleyian. Bachelor's degree in Theology and Biblical Sciences, Bachelor's degree in Psychology (Honors), University Professor, Senior Coach. Founder and Director of INEA International Institute, Mission Children, and Christian Psychology. Doctorate in Psychology and Neuroscience. Doctorate in Philosophy and Education. Author. www.psicologaana.com draanagkm@gmail.com www.facebook.com/DraAnaGKM

Ana María Cohen de Carballeda. Advanced theological studies. Educator. Psychological Consultant. Bachelor's degree in Journalism. Speaker and Author. adecarballeda@gmail.com

Ariel G. Gutiérrez. Pastor. Bachelor's and Master's degree in Religious Studies. arigugut@yahoo.com.ar

Cintia Puleo. Medical Doctor. Specialized in Child Psychiatry and Forensic Medicine. Garrahan Hospital. cintiapuleo@gmail.com

Gisela Daiana Vespa. Psychological Consultant. Bachelor's degree in Psychopedagogy. Bachelor's degree in Theology. Educational Counselor. giselavespa@hotmail.com

Gustavo F. Romero. Pastor. Bachelor's degree in Christian Studies. Psychological Consultant. Facilitator in Parenting School. Diplomas in Cognitive-Behavioral Approach and Couples Therapy. Specialization in anxiety, stress, and depression disorders. Founder of the Causa De Vida Foundation. prgustavoromero@gmail.com www.palabrasdedios.com.ar

María del Carmen García. Bachelor's degree in Psychology (UBA). Professor of Literature. Writer. Speaker. marianoval79@hotmail.com

Silvia Waisel. Bachelor's degree in Psychology (UBA) - Specialist in adult, adolescent, and child clinical psychology. waizelsilvia@gmail.com

Stella García. Bachelor's degree in Psychology. Diploma in Applied Positive Psychology. Professor. Researcher. lic.stellagarcia@gmail.com

Victoria Amorina Burgenik. Therapeutic Companion. Specialized in disability and school integration. alegriaporsiempre1@gmail.com

Yolanda Patricia Weigandt. Psychological Consultant. Family Advisor. Diploma in PNIE (Neuroscience and Emotional Intelligence Program). Bachelor's degree in Theology. yopawei@hotmail.com

OTHER BOOKS BY THE AUTHOR

https://a.co/ba60k59

https://a.co/dMqEbcT

https://a.co/2SOHho7

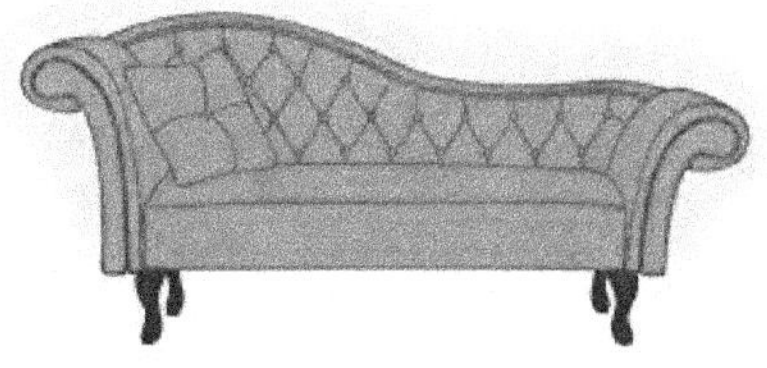

https://a.co/5Al55DI

https://a.co/d/ejQH10P

https://a.co/d/hdy7ne4

https://a.co/d/hdy7ne4

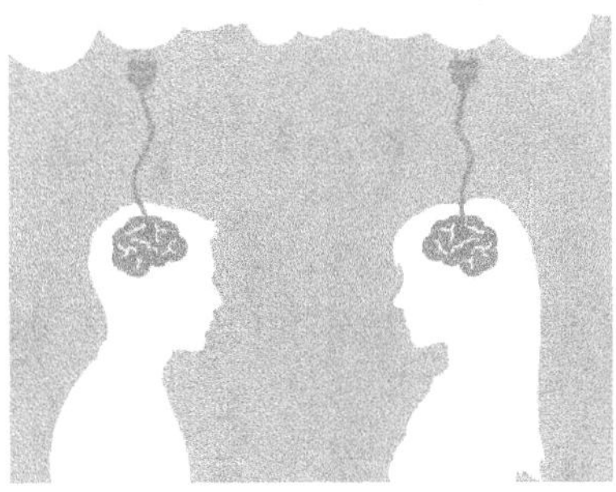

https://a.co/d/gPjFurF

Index

Chapter 11